GITTINOMIC$

ROSS GITTINS

GITTINOMIC$

Living the good life without money stress,
overwork and joyless consumption

ALLEN&UNWIN

For Claudia, love of my life

First published in 2007

Allen & Unwin
83 Alexander Street
Crows Nest NSW 2065
Australia
Phone: (61 2) 8425 0100
Fax: (61 2) 9906 2218
Email: info@allenandunwin.com
Web: www.allenandunwin.com

National Library of Australia
Cataloguing-in-Publication entry:

Gittins, Ross.
   Gittinomics : living the good life without money stress,
   overwork and joyless consumption

   Bibliography.
   ISBN 978 1 74175 092 8.

   1. Cost and standard of living – Australia – Popular works.
   2. Quality of life – Economic aspects – Australia. I.
   Title.

339.420994

Set in 11.5/17 pt Bembo by Midland Typesetters, Australia
Printed by Griffin Press, Adelaide

10 9 8 7 6 5 4

Contents

Home economics:
An introduction

At first blush this book isn't much about economics. The key topics of macro-economics—inflation, unemployment, interest rates, the current account deficit—rate only a passing mention. But appearances can be deceptive. This book is about the very essence of economics: you and your everyday life. Whereas much of economics tends to view 'the economy' from an aeroplane— the top-down view, in which the outline of the economic system becomes apparent, but the people who inhabit it appear no bigger than ants—this book takes a bottom-up view, in which the people are life size and the way they and 'the system' interact is the subject of study.

The great English economist Alfred Marshall called economics the study of mankind in the ordinary business of life. And the

GITTINOMIC$

American economist Herb Stein famously defined gross national product as what ensues when 100 million people get up in the morning and go to work. It's this 'home economics' that's our subject matter: work, leisure and the shortage of time, homes and housework, buying and saving, mothers and their kids, kids and their education, not to mention happiness and the things that may threaten it—crime, taxation, health and ageing. Are such matters mundane, straightforward, of little import? Hardly. They're the stuff of life. They dominate our waking hours, they're the way most of us earn our income and the way all of us spend it. When you break down The Economy, they're what you're left with. And they're not working too well.

Economics is about equilibrium, but many of us find our lives are out of balance. We're doing more of the things that don't satisfy us—don't yield lasting 'utility', as economists put it—and less of the things that do. That's partly because we don't always know what we want, or want what would be best for us, and partly because the things that matter most to us are things that offer the commercial world little opportunity to turn a dollar. Thus we spend much of our time running interference—trying to avoid being corralled by the strictures of demanding bosses or sidetracked by the blandishments of self-serving marketing.

So this book has a mission—or two. First, to help you understand how the economy around you works, how it's changing, how it impinges on your freedom of action—but also to expose the propaganda, the mistaken conventional wisdom, the tricks and illusions, the seeming constraints that aren't real. Second, to do what economics is supposed to do: help you maximise your utility.

Home economics

Avoid being taken in by the fashions and orthodoxies of our time. Take control of your life, be an instigator, not a victim, do less of what doesn't satisfy you and more of what does. Is this a self-help book? Sure.

You should know that my father was a preacher—a Salvation Army sky pilot, in fact. He had things he wanted to say to the world, and I have inherited the same failing. This book is the summation of most of the things I've wanted to say to the world after more than 30 years as an economic journalist on *The Sydney Morning Herald* and, latterly, *The Age* in Melbourne. It's built on many of the columns I've written. What do all those columns add up to? If you really want to know, keep reading.

The thing that's kept me going though all those years is an abiding curiosity about how the world works—and an equal desire to rush to tell my readers of any discovery I've made. I'm fascinated by the study of how people behave—what makes them do what they do—and have always focused that fascination on the ordinary business of life. The world is changing—probably more rapidly and comprehensively than at most times in our history—but sometimes in ways that aren't easily apparent from close up. It's the great privilege of the journalist to be among the first to draw attention to those changes and assay the first judgments of their significance.

Of course, over 30 years my opinions have changed—as has my view of my role as a commentator. For many years, while I was mastering the mysteries of economics, I saw my role as not just explaining conventional economics to my readers but convincing them of the merits of economic rationalism. The more I understood it, however, the more aware I became of its limitations. So these days I see my job as providing readers with a critique of economics—just as a theatre critic provides a critique of plays—acknowledging its strengths but also pointing out its weaknesses. I'm a journalist, first and foremost, and my loyalty is to my readers, not the economics profession.

In the chapters that follow you'll find various demonstrations of the strengths of conventional economics. The much-revered 'market forces' aren't as omnipresent and omnipotent as we're often asked to believe but, by the same token, they're more prevalent and powerful than most people appreciate. Take the deregulation of the banks which, we were assured, would increase competition and thereby reduce the interest rates they charge. Well, it took longer than expected, but it happened. The banks' interest margin—the gap between the interest rate they pay on deposits and the rate they charge their borrowers—is a percentage point or two narrower than it used to be, partly because of increased competition between the banks themselves but also because of a new source of competition from the new breed of non-bank mortgage lenders.

Though bank deregulation began as long ago as the mid-1980s, it took additional measures by the Reserve Bank to bring competition to the market for credit cards—in just the past year or two. Now, various institutions are offering cards with interest rates up to 6 percentage points lower than we're used to. But there's an important point to remember about the wonders of 'competition'—it's a double-sided exercise. You don't get banks fighting each other for business unless you also get customers picking and choosing between banks. When most of us can't be bothered shopping around, none of us is likely to benefit from much competition.

Merchants won't cut their profit margins unless they're obliged to, of course, and most customers are oblivious to many of the little tricks they use to maximise their profits. One such device is 'price discrimination'—charging different prices to different classes of customer. How does this practice make profits higher rather than lower? Conventional economics does a good job of explaining how.

Some of the big decisions concerning our kids' educations—Is it still worth it to get a uni education? Is it smart to pay off HECS as quickly as possible? How attractive is the discount for paying HECS up-front?—are just the kind of questions economics is designed to answer. As you'll see in Chapter 4, the answers are 'of course it is', 'no it's not' and 'quite—but only if you're a dad who wants to do it anyway'.

There's one area where a bit of elementary economics would do wonders, but is commonly regarded as far from the economist's domain: crime. For a start, more hard-headed rational analysis and less emotion would help. Too many of the crime solutions the public proposes—and politicians take up—seem intended to gratify people's fears or resentments rather than get results. Why else would people who get so stirred up about an issue be so uninterested in knowing what works and what doesn't? And then, of course, there's economics' simplest but most useful contribution to policy-making: the concept of opportunity cost—the notion that money doesn't grow on trees and each dollar you spend can only be spent once, so make sure you choose wisely. Opportunity cost reminds us that, even when we've established that putting more cops on the beat actually does reduce crime, there's a further question to ask: is there another way of spending the money that would do a better job of reducing crime for the same cost? We should be searching for cost-effectiveness in the fight against crime, just as in anything else governments do with taxpayers' money.

So much for conventional economics. But before we give up on economics, is there some *unconventional* economics that could help us decipher the inner workings of everyday life? I've been much attracted to a relatively new school of economic thought known as 'behavioural economics', which uses the discoveries and methods of psychology to solve economic problems. Where conventional economics confidently assumes us to be 'rational' in our decisions—to be always acting with clear-headed self-interest—the behavioural economists know our decision-making to be often far from rational. Conventional economics is notorious for its poor record in predicting human behaviour and I suspect its mistaken assumption of rationality does much to explain that poor performance. But there's much predictability in our non-rational approach to life, so behavioural economics has many useful insights to offer.

You'll find various references to psychologists' experiments and much use of behaviouralist thinking in this book. For instance, experiments reveal how much trouble we have making choices when buying things and how, when the choices get too tough, we often simply avoid them. And the work of psychologists has done much to reveal television-watching for what it is: a surprisingly unsatisfying activity that, taken to extremes, can leave us in a state of mild depression.

Happiness—alias utility—used to be the special subject of economics before the profession took a wrong turning. These days it's the object of much scientific inquiry, but with psychologists dominating the field and only marginal participation by economists. But give it time and the psychologists will lead the economists back to where they should be.

Studies of happiness and other psychological research have done much to modify our understanding of the role of work. The unemployed, for instance, miss the work more than they miss the money. And whereas economists obsess about raising the productivity of workers, one day economists, politicians and business people will understand the benefit to be gained from 'job enrichment'—making work more satisfying.

Behaviouralist thinking is useful when we seek to explain the veritable collapse in household saving. I think part of the explanation lies in the way advances in technology have made money less tangible. These days, our wages come to us as figures on our bank statement, while we pay bills by computer and buy things with bits of plastic. Were we the unemotional calculator-machines conventional economics assumes us to be, this would make not a whit of difference to our behaviour. In reality, I suspect it leads at least some of us to spend more than we would have had we held our hard-earned cash in our hands.

Then there's the puzzle of why so few of those who don't pay their credit card bill in full each month—and so never gain any days of free credit—have switched to the cards the banks offered at significantly lower interest rates but with no free credit. I suspect this reluctance to switch was a combination of self-delusion and a failed attempt at self-discipline. These people were always telling themselves they'd escape their debt trap by making the effort to pay in full next month, and so wanted to stay with the card that rewarded such behaviour with up to 55 days' free credit.

You can see a yawning gap between conventional and behavioural economics in their rival attitudes to tax indexation. The conventional, rational view is that the politicians' failure to index the income-tax scales each year is what permits bracket creep—making us all victims of 'the secret tax of inflation'— so that ending this blatant injustice should be a high priority. But the pollies show little interest in tax indexation and, quite frankly, there's little pressure from the public for such a reform.

Why? Because, I suspect, of a fundamental contradiction in the public's attitudes towards government finances. On one hand, we hate the idea of tax increases and implacably oppose any new tax. On the other, our demands for increased government spending know no bounds. So the pollies keep bracket creep up their sleeves as their not-so-secret weapon for helping them square this circle. It's as though, in the unwritten contract between politicians and the electorate, there's a clause requiring tax increases to be as inconspicuous as possible.

And we do know the public quite likes an illusion. We like the idea that, under Medicare, using public hospitals is 'free', while bulk-billing makes visiting the doctor 'free'. Nothing's free, of course; we all pay through our taxes. But those two illusions do much to account for the undying popularity of Medicare.

Home economics

But unorthodox economics can take us only so far in countering the weaknesses of conventional economics. And at many points in the book I find it necessary to warn you of those weaknesses—which, of course, is a backhanded compliment to economic rationalism, the dominant ideology of our times.

When it comes to something as simple as housework, conventional economics' great failing is to ignore it completely. So here we have the household sector of the economy—constituting five 'industries' pumping out accommodation, meals, child care, laundry and transport—that actually involves about 20 per cent more hours of work than the market sector, and the economics profession acts as though it doesn't exist. It's not part of GDP, so we can forget it. The two sectors trade with each other and compete with each other, but we can focus all our attention on one and ignore the other. Terrific.

Economic rationalism tells us the increased choice consumers now enjoy in a less regulated economy is an unmitigated blessing— a benefit to be set beside lower prices and better service. Well, of course, some choice is better than none. True. The deeper truth, however—one that seems to have escaped most economists, perhaps because they leave the shopping to others—is that ordinary mortals frequently find choice confusing and discomforting. This makes choice an easy device for businesses to use to increase profits and avoid competing on price or service.

Some people might imagine that economics has little connection with the subject of time. In truth, time and economics are inextricably linked, and the object of economics can easily be restated as 'helping people overcome the scarcity of time'. There's just one problem: economics' answer is to find ways to cram more and more into every hour, to make our lives move faster and faster. One assumption of economics so basic it's rarely mentioned is: more is better. It's an understandable mistake. But in our ever-more-frantic world, the beginning of wisdom is to understand that sometimes less is more.

The thing that worries me most about economics, however, is the way it's got itself sidetracked into the mindless pursuit of consumption. As we've seen, economics started out with the goal of helping people maximise their utility—their satisfaction, subjective wellbeing or happiness, call it what you will. It went astray when it decided that, since utility was impossible to measure, it would cut to the chase and concentrate simply on helping societies maximise their production and consumption of goods and services. Thus have we acquired a profession devoted to elevating consumerism to the supreme objective of our lives, an objective to which all other more social or spiritual goals should be sacrificed.

Looking around, you could be forgiven for thinking the economists had managed to pick the mood of our times with precision. Our devotion to consumption is so great at present that households' spending exceeds their income—our saving is negative. Many of us are working long hours to make the money to buy the stuff we suppose will make us happy. Even so, I doubt that, in their obsession with consumption, the economists have understood what's driving us. Look more deeply at the things we're buying and you see that, in many cases, we're trying to acquire something more than just stuff.

Home economics

A 10-year-old Toyota gets us from A to B reliably enough—and I should know—but when we buy a brand-new European model, we're hoping to come by something more than a faster, smoother or more comfortable ride. What is it? Social status. We're seeking to signal—to make conspicuous—our superior position in the social order. Look at our spending on clothes, entertaining, the private schools we send our kids to, the homes and suburbs we choose to live in and much else, and you see how often we're trying to buy status as well as functionality. Much of the demonstration of our superior status arises, of course, simply from the very much higher prices of the brands and models we prefer—referred to by the (unorthodox) economist who coined the term as 'positional goods'.

This search for status along with consumption is something to which most conventional economists are oblivious. As well they may be. Why? Because, from the viewpoint of society rather than the individual, the pursuit of status is a pointless exercise. In a status race, as much as in an arms race, there must always be as many losers as winners. So if what we're all really after is status rather than satisfying avarice, economics can't help us and economists have been whipping us on to no useful end. They're certainly not doing much to enhance society's *total* utility.

Business people are always trying to make us feel guilty about taking time off—public holidays, four whole weeks of annual leave (shocking!), even our reluctance to work on weekends. Conventional economics—or rather, *textbook* economics—does a good job of countering such silliness. Why? Because economics is about helping people maximise their utility or satisfaction, and you don't need to be smart to see that leisure brings us much utility. Trouble is, in the hands of conventional economists, the value of leisure often doesn't make it beyond the pages of elementary texts. Anyhow, that's one of the sub-themes of this book: leisure is good, not bad, so we should ignore the business propagandists and enjoy more of it rather than less.

But while economic theory does acknowledge the utility we derive from leisure, the other side of the proposition's wrong. The theory assumes leisure brings utility because it's not work, since we all know work brings *dis*-utility. Really? While that's true for some people and some types of work, for most people most of the time, work too brings utility. Indeed, many of us derive our very identity from our occupation. And have economists not heard of job satisfaction? Of course they have, as they're quick to protest. Trouble is, their model hasn't, and most of them seem oblivious to the way this wrong assumption taints the policies they recommend and the predictions they make.

The economists' model tends to focus on factors such as demand and supply and price, while ignoring the role of economic 'institutions'—not just the organisations, but also the laws, customs and norms of behaviour that surround and support particular markets.

That's what economists (and business people and politicians, too) can't see when they think of mothers in the paid workforce. The women want paid maternity leave? Goodness, have you any idea of the extra cost that would impose on employers? And they'd have to pass it on in higher prices, you know. It's true, they would. But the same could have been said against a host of long-standing imposts that have passed without question: the 40-hour week, annual leave, long-service leave, even sick leave.

What's missing is an understanding of the way the institutions of the labour market have been shaped over the centuries to meet the needs of men, but not women. Through almost all that time we didn't bother educating our girls to levels that would allow them to make a highly skilled contribution to the paid workforce. And now all that's changed—now that women, their families and the taxpayer are investing heavily in girls' education—economic good sense as much as sexual equality says we must remodel the institutions of the labour market to make them more accommodating of the requirements of the child-bearing sex. If you can't see that, you're not much of an economist.

I'm convinced the educational emancipation of women— and the consequent feminisation of the workforce—constitutes the most profound economic and social change of our lifetime. As I've said, it's the great privilege of a journalist to be among the first to chronicle the major social changes, and this book records much of my efforts. I'm supposed to list the dreaded Globalisation as prominent among the great trends of our times, but I'll spare you and subsume that ugly word under two less off-putting headings: the advance of technology and the rise of hyper-materialism.

There's nothing new about new technology, of course. New and better machines, and new and better ways of doing things, have been coming thick and fast since the onset of the industrial revolution in the early 1800s. And there's nothing new about changing technology leading to changes in the way we lead our lives. Technology illustrates my point that the most high-powered and high-flying subjects in economics get their exalted status from nothing more than the extent of their influence on our daily lives. And it seems fair to say that when you put computerisation together with recent advances in telecommunications you've got pretty extensive and rapid changes in the way we work and live.

Similarly, there's nothing new about materialism. It's long been with us, and we're all materialists to a greater or lesser extent. In writing about it, I'm certainly not meaning to imply that you're infected by the bug and I'm not. However, as you'll see, a case can be made that we're living through a period of *heightened* materialism, where politicians stress the primacy of economic growth above all things, economists are on top in the world of policy advice, and business people are particularly aggressive and convinced of their moral authority.

While I'm no stranger to the discussion of social trends, I confess it wasn't until I was pulling this book together that I realised how much the key trends overlap, interact and reinforce each other. Starting with the educational and economic emancipation of women, it explains why housework—and the amount of it men do—has become such a bone of contention in many homes and why so many of us are feeling so much more pressed for time. The addition of mothers' incomes helps explain why many families are able to spend more on their children's education and why our kids both need to and are able to leave home later. Of course, the fact that girls are now educated as highly as boys adds to the need for greater spending on our kids' education, as well as explaining why girls are leaving home later.

Turning to technology, computerisation helps explain the growth in the white-collar jobs that so many women have taken up. Technology has both made housework easier and greatly affected the way we spend our leisure time, without leaving us any more time to spare. Technological advances explain much of the never-ending increase in our spending on health care. Improvements in medical technology explain why people are living longer, while it was contraceptive technology that made possible the decline in the birth rate. Put those two together and you've explained the ageing of the population. For good measure, advances in technology explain why more of us need to spend longer in the education system learning to handle the stuff.

Our heightened materialism explains many other changes. To some extent it may help motivate mothers to take paid employment. It helps explain our rapid take-up of new technology around the home, while technological advance produces much of the increased productivity that allows us to produce and consume more stuff. The longer hours some of us are working help us earn more money to buy more stuff—which is true whether the longer hours are voluntary or involuntary. The era of hyper-materialism explains why so many parts of our lives have been commercialised—sport and other aspects of our leisure, including the weekend. The higher incomes we're enjoying as part of the consumerist project help finance our increased spending on health and education—including our growing preference for private schools and having more kids go on to uni. And though the crime wave is now clearly receding, its rise coincided with the onset of heightened materialism. It may not be drawing too long a bow to see all of these as linked in some way.

But enough scene-setting. Let's get down to cases.

PART ONE

FAMILY FINANCES

CHAPTER 1
The changing workforce

We're all conscious of how rapidly the world of work is changing. And it's true, it is. The strange thing, however, is that it's not changing the way we think it is. We think we know, for instance, that everyone with a full-time job is working much longer hours, and a lot of the extra overtime is unpaid. But this conventional wisdom's inaccurate in several respects. Most of us are conscious that managers and professionals have been getting much bigger pay rises than people in less-skilled occupations. That's as true as it seems. And here's a highly significant change in the workforce that few of us have noticed: it's growing at the top and at the bottom, but shrinking in the middle. Clearly, we need to take a closer look at the evidence.

According to a study of longer working hours, included in the Bureau of Statistics' *Australian Social Trends 2003*, the great epidemic of overwork is subsiding. Of late, we're working less, not more. In any case, the most recent research suggests the whole story's been a bit overdone. We've been given an exaggerated impression of how widespread the overwork is, how much of it is unpaid, how unhappy workers are about it and how much effect it's having on family life.

It's true that, on average, Australia's full-time workers are working longer hours than they did 20 years ago. Between the late 1970s and the late 1990s, average hours increased from fewer than 40 to more than 41 hours a week. But, although the news has been slow getting through, average hours stopped increasing after 2000. And in the following five years they fell a little, so that they're now back to 40 hours and 40 minutes a week. I guess you don't have to try hard to convince most of us we're 'overworked and under-paid'. And when you've got a story that fits people's preconceived notions so well, it's tempting not to complicate things with inconvenient facts.

But when you delve into the figures you're soon disabused of the notion that we're *all* working longer hours these days. It remains true that about half of all full-time workers are putting in 40 hours a week or less. And it turns out that most of the overall increase in average hours has been caused by a small minority of workers—10 per cent—working very much longer hours than they did. Since 1982, the proportion of full-timers working 50 hours or more a week has gone from 20 per cent to 30 per cent. (But even here that 30 per cent is down from what it was a few years ago.)

So, if we're not *all* working a lot longer hours, who is exactly? Well, for a start, it's almost twice as likely to be men as women.

The changing workforce

About 19 per cent of women work 50 hours a week or more, compared with 35 per cent of men. But the next point is that it's more likely to be the self-employed than employees. The 2001 census shows that 57 per cent of self-employed business people work 50 hours or more, compared with 23 per cent of employees.

The people working very long hours, self-employed and employees, tend to be in occupations involving high levels of responsibility, high earnings and no awards or agreements specifying standard working hours. According to the 2001 census, the occupational category where long hours are most common is—surprise, surprise—managers and administrators. For instance, 65 per cent of general managers work 50 hours or more. And among farmers—most of whom would own their property—it's 76 per cent. But when you come to a managerial job done mainly by female employees—child-care coordinators—the proportion drops to 24 per cent.

Among professionals you have 65 per cent of (mainly self-employed) medical specialists working 50 hours or more, and 57 per cent of GPs. Among secondary school teachers, however, the proportion falls to 31 per cent, and among registered nurses, just 12 per cent. Among associate professionals you have (largely self-employed) hotel and motel managers on 73 per cent and shop managers on 52 per cent, but police officers on 18 per cent. More than 60 per cent of taxi drivers and chauffeurs work 50 hours or more, as do 47 per cent of truck drivers. Many of these people would be self-employed.

In 2000 the Bureau of Statistics asked employees (note that) how they felt about the hours they were working. Among those working 49 hours or more a week, almost two-thirds said they preferred to continue working the same hours for the same pay. Only 11 per cent said they'd prefer to work fewer hours for less pay and these were pretty much offset by the 8 per cent who'd prefer to work longer hours for more pay. Among employees working between 35 and 48 hours a week, the proportion wanting to work longer hours for more pay jumped to 19 per cent.

So let's have a little bit less about how the wicked capitalist system is forcing us to work longer hours than we want. A lot of us are doing it for the money. And that brings us to overtime— paid and unpaid. Here we're looking only at employees, obviously. There was little change in the proportion of employees regularly working overtime, the number of overtime hours worked, or the proportion of employees working unpaid overtime between 1993 and 2000, though the proportion regularly working overtime rose to 37 per cent in the three years to 2003.

Of those full-time employees who regularly worked overtime, only 38 per cent were paid for it by the hour. But here's the bit that gets less publicity: a further 30 per cent were paid indirectly, as part of their salary package or with time off in lieu, etc. Admittedly, that still leaves just under a third who weren't paid. But even here unpaid overtime is most common among professionals and managers. For instance, a high proportion of teachers complain their overtime is unpaid. To me, however, this complaint is misdirected. Teachers are professionals. The point is not that they should be signing timebooks and getting time-and-a-half, it's that they're not being paid well like other professionals (with extra hours taken for granted as part of the package).

The changing workforce

Now let's look at all the hours put in by working families at a time when more wives have been working. In June 2002, two-income families *without* dependants spent an average of a combined 62 hours a week in paid employment, up almost two hours from the figure in 1992. For those *with* dependants, however, the increase was only half an hour a week, to a combined 58 hours. And, although the proportions of couples who worked a combined 80 hours or more a week rose between 1992 and 1999 from 22 per cent to 29 per cent for those without kids, and from 17 per cent to 21 per cent for those with kids, since then the respective proportions have fallen, to 24 per cent and 17 per cent.

So, while no one's yet had time to tell you, the alleged epidemic of overwork has turned down. And the idea that it ever applied to most of us was always mistaken. But the study of working hours has deeper implications than you may imagine. For instance, have you ever looked at your reasonably healthy income and wondered where it all goes—why you don't have more to show for it? On the other hand, have you ever looked at a figure for the 'average household income', noted how small it seems and wondered how anyone could possibly get by on it?

A big part of the explanation for these mysteries of modern life lies in the nature of time. No matter how rich or poor we are, we all get an equal ration of time: 24 hours in a day, seven days in a week. That's hardly a blinding insight, but it's so obvious we often fail to take account of it. When you do take account of it, you realise that our equal ration of time is a great leveller between the seemingly well-off and the seeming battlers. It doesn't eliminate the gap, but it does reduce it more than we realise.

This tale is about neither the genuinely rich (tycoons like the late Kerry Packer and the people at the top of Australia's 100 or 200 biggest public companies) nor the genuinely poor (people wholly dependent on government benefits). Rather, we'll limit our comparisons to the great bulk of working middle-class families. Within the bounds of normal working families, the way to be well-off is to have a well-paying job—a job with the sort of salary that, as we're constantly being reminded, has been rising strongly for the past decade or more.

But here's the first point: the people pulling in those big salaries are, as a general rule, working much longer hours than people in lesser-paid jobs. In May 2004, the average earnings of male full-time workers in the top occupational category—managers and administrators—were $1609 a week. This was twice as much as the earnings of men in the lowest category—labourers—of $786 a week. But now consider the official figures for the hours worked in February 2006 by men with full-time jobs. More than half of managers worked 50 or more hours a week, whereas only 18 per cent of labourers worked that long. (Thirty-two per cent of professionals and associate professionals worked that many hours, but only 23 per cent of tradesmen.) So, while it's undoubtedly true that *hourly* rates of pay are higher among managers and professionals than they are among tradespeople and labourers, it's also true that the longer hours put in by people in the more-skilled occupations do much to explain their higher incomes.

The next question is: how do you get to be in the top 20 per cent of *household* income? One way is to have a tycoon or a CEO in your family, but the way most families attain that position is far more mundane: they have both partners working—and, no doubt, both working full time. Bureau of Statistics figures for 2003/04 show that the average after-tax income of the top 20 per cent of households was $1886 a week. This was 2.4 times the income of households in the middle 20 per cent of households—$790 a week. But if you divide those sums by the average number of people employed in each household, the gap between them falls to 35 per cent. Putting it another way, the average after-tax income per employed person was just $212 a week more in the top households than in the middle households.

See the point? The main way some families get to have a lot more income than others is to put in a lot more hours of paid work. And the other side of this—the side we tend to forget—is that they give up a lot more hours of free time. So here we have a major phenomenon of modern life. Ordinary working families can be divided into two groups: the cash rich/time poor and the cash poor/time rich. Given the choice, I guess most families would opt to be in the former category.

But my point is that, when you examine it, the gap between the two groups isn't as wide as it appears. Why not? Because the cash rich/time poor families end up having to pay other people to do many of the jobs around the house they don't have time to do for themselves. Those official figures provided a wealth of detail on just what it is families spend their incomes on. The top 20 per cent of households spend twice what the middle households spend on painters. They spend more than twice as much on electricians.

They spend twice as much on fast food and take-away meals and more than twice as much on 'household services', such as cleaning, ironing, lawnmowing and rubbish removal. But while we're in the garden, note this: they spend a lot less on the purchase of lawnmowers.

The top 20 per cent spend almost four times as much on drycleaning—probably not just because of their lack of time, but also because working wives have to worry more about their appearance. (They spend well over twice as much on women's clothing.) Not surprisingly, they spend almost three times as much on child care.

They spend about twice as much on the purchase of motor cars—which is high when you remember that they're more likely to have access to a company car. Part of the explanation may be that they're inclined to buy flasher cars, but another part would be their greater need to have two. They spend twice as much on having their vehicles serviced, but only 45 per cent more on the separate purchase of vehicle parts (less time to fool around fixing cars). And they spend 2.5 times as much on taxis.

So, if you're a two-income family, pulling in big bucks but wondering why you don't have more to show for it, those comparisons help explain why. Much of your extra income is lost through having to pay people to do things for you while you work. And if you wonder how people on much lower incomes get by—that's how. They're able to maintain a higher standard of living than you'd expect because they have more time to do their own chores.

But now let's look at a different aspect of work: how the nature of jobs and occupations has changed. In 2002, Mark Cully, then of the National Institute of Labour Studies at Flinders University,

The changing workforce

studied the change during the 15 years between the censuses of 1986 and 2001. He found that the total number of jobs (full-time and part-time) grew by 1.8 million to 8.1 million, an increase of 28 per cent. But what kind of jobs were they? Well, consistent with all the hype, no fewer than one million of the extra jobs were in the highest-skilled occupations: managers, professionals and associate professionals. Contrary to the conventional wisdom, however, 700 000 of the new jobs—about four in 10—were in unskilled or semi-skilled occupations in the services sector. Almost 200 000 of those jobs, for instance, were for shop assistants.

This confirmed the position of shop assistants as the largest of our 340 occupations. We have 475 000 of them, followed by 200 000 secretaries or personal assistants and almost 200 000 cleaners. Other less-skilled occupations that have seen strong growth include (in descending order) child-care workers, waiters, special-care workers, sales reps, receptionists, storepersons and checkout operators. So forget the notion that we'll soon be running out of jobs for those lacking academic qualifications. Experience suggests we'll always have plenty of less-skilled (though poorly paid) jobs in the services sector.

But here's the disturbing bit: the 15 years saw almost no net growth in the number of middle-level skilled jobs—jobs that require post-school training, but not a uni degree. The most glaring example is qualified tradespeople. Had jobs in the trades merely preserved their share of total employment, they would have grown by 300 000. In fact, their number fell by 13 000. Employment is down in almost all trades: electricians, telco repairmen, carpenters, bricklayers, butchers, printers, upholsterers, panel beaters and all kinds of metal trades. At the same time, employment's been stagnant among advanced clerical and service workers—jobs such as insurance agents, desktop publishing operators and bank tellers (with bank loans officers being the only category of strong growth).

Do you see what's happened? We've experienced huge growth in the most highly skilled occupations and surprisingly strong growth in the least skilled occupations, but stagnation or decline in ordinary skilled employment. It's as though the skills structure of Australia's workforce is being hollowed out. In his researches, Mr Cully was struck by the 'tremendous change in the occupational composition of employment'. Among the 340 occupations, 64 at least doubled in size, whereas 84 declined. Managers, for instance, now account for almost one in 10 of the workforce. Just about every class of manager has grown (in descending order): sales and marketing managers, information technology managers, production managers and distribution managers. Only among farm managers has there been a fall.

But the growth in managers is dwarfed by the growth in professionals—who now account for almost 20 per cent of the workforce. We've seen outstanding growth in the number of professionals in computing, accounting, marketing, advertising and business analysis. Growth has been strong among the associate professionals, too: project administrators, financial dealers, customer service managers and investment advisers.

The challenge is to explain the strange 'hourglass' shape that the skills structure of the workforce is adopting. Mr Cully speculates that several different trends have been at work. First is the continuation

The changing workforce

of the long-standing trend for advances in technology to make the agricultural, mining, manufacturing and construction sectors more mechanised and less labour-intensive. The computerisation of manufacturing goes a long way towards explaining the decline in blue-collar job opportunities, particularly for men—the decline in jobs for tradespeople, intermediate production and transport workers (machine operators, printing hands, forestry workers and suchlike), process workers and labourers.

At the same time, it seems that advances in machining (such as computer-aided design and manufacture) are 'deskilling' employment in manufacturing, so those jobs that remain are less likely to be performed by tradespeople and more likely by tradespeople's mates. As an example, the number of wood machinists and turners fell by 1700, whereas the number of wood-processing machine operators rose by 1900. Such a trend sees job opportunities in manufacturing moving from the middle of the skills distribution down towards the bottom.

Within the services sector, however, the trend seems to have been running the other way: jobs in the middle are being replaced by jobs higher up. This is the trend to 'professionalise' occupations by requiring university qualifications. The classic example is nursing. The past 15 years have seen a 32 per cent fall in enrolled nurses, but a 22 per cent increase in registered nurses. Librarians are another example. Library assistants are down 8400, but library technicians (a para-professional category) are up 4600. But the doozy of them all is employee relations. Personnel clerks are down 1400, but human resource professionals are up 31 000 and human resource managers are up 19 000(!).

Yet another trend helping to explain the hole in the middle of the skills distribution is the spread of computers through offices, which has reduced the demand for routine clerical functions. For instance, the 69 000 halving in the number of keyboard operators (formerly known as typists) has occurred as office workers of all skill levels have learnt to use desktop computers.

To explain the growth in less–skilled occupations, however, we need to turn to the growing affluence of working families, particularly two–income professional couples. On one hand we have their increased spending on luxuries and leisure activities helping to account for the growth in waiters, travel agents, personal care consultants, fitness instructors and gaming workers. On the other we have couples paying outsiders to do their housework and thus helping to explain the growth in child-care workers, cleaners and handypersons.

Finally, we have our increased preference for late–night and weekend shopping helping to explain the remarkable growth of 200 000 in shop assistants and 30 000 in checkout operators. (Note, however, that most of these jobs are part-time.) So, although it's true that most of the jobs—and, certainly, most of the better-paid jobs—are going increasingly to university graduates, the full story is far more complicated. There'll always be jobs for the less skilled, if only because managers and professionals can afford to pay for personal service, but the middle ground is disappearing.

But while we're on the subject of work, there's something else that needs saying. I think that, in the present era of turbo-charged capitalism, work is one of the things we're getting badly wrong. The conventional economists' model assumes work is a

The changing workforce

'disutility'—an unpleasant means to a pleasant end: money and all you can buy with it. But the work of the psychologists and economists studying happiness confirms what most of us already know, that work plays a very important part in our happiness and that a lot of our happiness actually comes from the work we do.

It provides a lot of our self-identity (how often have you explained aspects of your character or behaviour by reference to your occupation?), our friendships and our feelings about the purpose and value of our lives. So work turns out to be both a means to an end (as the economists assume) and an end in itself (as the economists don't assume). Work has intrinsic benefits; it's good for its own sake. We seem to be animals that are built to work, and without work—even the much-reduced amount of work that an 80-year-old grandmother in an extended household might find to 'make herself useful'—we have trouble being happy.

Let's look at some of the research. In a lecture series he delivered in 2003, Professor Richard Layard of the London School of Economics summarised what other economists have learnt from extensive surveys in many countries. On average, the loss of happiness suffered by people who are unemployed is three times greater than the fall in happiness suffered by people whose family income drops by a third relative to average income. So not having a job when you should have one is much worse than suffering a sudden drop in income. (Note that this separates the effect of being unemployed from the effect of the income you lose when you lose your job. That comes on top of what you feel about not working.) And, on average, those people who feel insecure about retaining their job suffer a loss of happiness relative to those who do feel secure that's 50 per cent greater than the loss of happiness suffered by people whose income drops by a third.

Research by Andrew Oswald, professor of economics at the University of Warwick in England, confirms that having a lot of job security is important to feeling a high degree of satisfaction with your job. What other factors affect job satisfaction? Well, people with relatively high incomes or university degrees tend to get more satisfaction, according to Professor Oswald's surveys. And women tend to be more satisfied than men. The self-employed tend to be more satisfied, as do people who work in a small workplace. The amount of time you spend commuting affects job satisfaction, and working at home tends to lead to higher satisfaction. Against that, however, a job that involves dealing with people tends to bring even higher satisfaction.

It's well known that job satisfaction is significantly affected by how much say you have over what you do and the way you do it. One famous study by Michael Marmot and colleagues even found that the degree of control you have in your job affects your health. It's not the bosses who feel the stress, it's the people at the bottom, who're always under orders. Professor Oswald finds that tight deadlines and high-speed work are bad for satisfaction. But who controls the pace of work is critical. When customers control it, that's good for job satisfaction. And when your colleagues do, that's OK. But when the pace is controlled by production targets that's bad, and when it's controlled by the boss that's very bad. On the brighter side, small freedoms—such as being able to move your desk or change the lighting—are very good.

The changing workforce

The point is that although nicer or smarter bosses worry about the job satisfaction of their workers, all the pressures on them in recent years have been running the other way, encouraging them to forget their workers' feelings and treat them as packhorses to be worked harder, and as costs to be cut. While at one level every economist knows work can be satisfying, that doesn't stop them urging 'reforms' on governments and businesses, inspired by a model that assumes all work is an unpleasant way of gaining money and that the unemployed are to be envied for all their leisure time. Under the influence of conventional economists obsessed by the goal of making us richer faster, for the past 20 years we've been labouring mightily to make work more efficient—more productive—oblivious to what that was doing to push workers into unemployment and make jobs less secure and less satisfying.

Sounds pretty topsy-turvy to me. And not a smart way to encourage people to work longer and retire later. It strikes me that a sensible way to respond to the labour shortages the retirement of the baby boomers will bring is for economists and politicians to join the push for 'job enrichment'.

CHAPTER 2
Women at work

When I left school in 1964, less than a third of women participated in the world of work; today it's well over half. Then, women held a quarter of the full-time jobs; today it's a third. In those days, part-time jobs represented less than 9 per cent of all jobs; today it's 28 per cent. And today, as then, women hold more than 70 per cent of those part-time jobs. So over the working lives of the baby boomers we've witnessed a quite remarkable social and economic change: the Feminisation of the Workforce.

The obvious question is, why? Why is it that an ever-growing number of women are returning to—or never really leaving— the paid workforce? To politicians as diverse as Paul Keating and John Howard, the answer is equally obvious: economic necessity. Mr Keating observed when he entered politics in the late 1960s that 'too many young married women are being forced out to work because of the high cost of living in this country'. All of Mr Howard's various efforts to give women the 'choice' to stay home with their kids have been built on the assumption that this is what they'd prefer to do if only they could afford it.

But I think the politicians are quite wrong. To me it's clear that mothers want to work to exploit their investment in a high level of education. They're interested in the money, sure, but they're also interested in having a career—which they see as the point of acquiring the education in the first place. Men have ambitions within the workforce and these days—surprise, surprise—so do women. I call it the economic emancipation of women, and it's probably the most profound economic and social shift of our lifetime.

Because this trend began so long ago—because we've grown up with it—we take it too cheaply. We don't appreciate its profundity, we don't understand its origins and we've yet to accept the further changes we need to make to come to terms with it. I think its origin lies in an attitude-switch among parents sometime in the 1960s, that girls are just as much entitled to an education as boys. Add the fact that girls have taken to education like ducks to water, and just look where we are today. The nationwide Year 12 retention rate for girls is 79 per cent, compared with 68 per cent for boys. Females now represent 55 per cent of all higher education students and 49 per cent of all vocational education and training students. Among the entire population of working age, women's share of those with post-school qualifications is 45 per cent—and counting.

It's this remarkable shift in the level of women's educational attainment that does most to explain the equally marked rise in their rate of participation in the labour force. It's what should convince us once and for all that they're not working just for the money. It should convince us that, these days and far into the future, virtually all young women will be seeking to fit a family in with an (interrupted) lifetime of paid employment—except, of course, for the growing minority who decide not to bother with a family at all.

We need to keep reminding ourselves of the big investment young women have made in their further education—the income forgone, the leisure time forgone and the HECS debt acquired— and the way this will influence their determination to keep working and extracting the full range of rewards from that investment: the money, the status and the psychic satisfactions. But there's another, more mercenary point we need to remember (and, since it *is* so mercenary, I can't understand why the economic rationalists haven't been ramming it down our throats this long time).

Even in these days of private schools and uni fees, it remains true that the great bulk of the direct cost of educating young people is borne by the community (the general taxpayer) rather than the individual or their family. The community does this partly because of our belief in the *intrinsic* benefits of education (a point too easily overlooked in these mercenary days), but also because we see it as an investment on the community's part. In other words, the better educated and trained we make the nation's workers, the richer we can expect the nation to become.

But here's the rub: it's now the case that *more than half* of all the nation spends on education and training is going on girls and women. So if many of those women are frustrated in their efforts to fully exploit their education in the paid workforce, it's not just those women and their families who suffer. The rest of us suffer, too. The community, having invested so heavily in women's education, allows much of the potential benefit from that investment to be lost when it stands by and allows so many women to be frustrated in their efforts to exploit their education.

Or think of it this way. Because men dominated the labour force for so long, we have a labour force whose institutions (laws and practices) were designed to accommodate men. But now, thanks to the economic emancipation of women—the democratisation of work—we discover that roughly half our workers are women. And it turns out that women have three characteristics that make them very different from men: they bear the children, breastfeed them and provide more than their fair share of the care. To date, we've hardly done much more than say 'Sorry, love, that's *your* problem'.

My point is, there are two good reasons why we need to get serious about remodelling our labour force institutions to accommodate the special needs of the reproductive sex. The first is, that's what half the population has shown by its behaviour it wants to happen. The female half of the electorate has been demonstrating for a long time that it wants a family *and* a career. (The wonder is that it's taking the politicians so long to get the message.) The second reason is that, for as long as it takes us to make the changes needed to juggle career and family more easily, the community will be wasting much of its investment in women's education.

So what should we be doing? Here's a partial list. We need to understand the extent to which the income tax and benefit system has been biased in favour of stay-at-home mums and so penalises those mothers who return to work. We need to think more clearly about fertility and what we could be doing to ensure its decline is reversed. We need to acknowledge the key role played by child-care arrangements and do a much better job of assisting them. Let's look at each of these in turn.

I'm sure you remember hearing people complain about how single-income families are obliged to pay a lot more income tax than families with the same income, but using two earners to get it. This perceived injustice arises because, under our system, people are taxed as individuals, not as part of a couple. And also because our tax scale is 'progressive', meaning that you lose a progressively higher *proportion* of your income in tax as your income rises. So family A, where the husband earns, say, $60 000 a year, while the wife stays home to mind the kids, ends up paying a lot more tax than family B, where both husband and wife work, each pulling in $30 000 a year. It's obvious that, whereas family A gets only one tax-free threshold (where you pay no tax on the first $6000 of your income), family B gets two—and also gets more of its joint income taxed at lower rates.

If you think that's unfair, you don't think it with more conviction than John Howard does—and, I suspect, Janette Howard. Since the time he was Treasurer in the Fraser Government, Mr Howard has believed that, to make the system fairer, single-income families really ought to be able to split their income between husband and wife for tax purposes. And you may not know it—it's never hit the headlines—but, in the 10 years he's been Prime Minister, he has worked untiringly to set things to rights.

Women at work

Consider this example, which comes from a 2004 paper by Patricia Apps, professor of economics at Sydney University. In 2003/04, a single-income family on $60 000 a year, with one child under five, paid net tax of $12 000. A similar family, with the same joint income but with each parent earning $30 000 a year, paid net tax of a little over $10 000. So in this case, the advantage of having two incomes and getting two tax-free thresholds etc. had been reduced to less than $1900 a year, or about $36 a week. In other words, we've come a long way towards where we'd be if single-income families were indeed allowed to split their income. In the jargon of tax economists, we've almost reached the point of having a 'joint' tax system.

Now consider this. As a result of the changes announced in the 2004 Federal Budget, the single-income family's net tax bill fell by $1560 a year, whereas the two-income family's net tax bill fell by only $600. So the latest changes reduced the gap in taxes paid by the two families by about half, to just $18 a week. In the process we moved even closer to a joint taxation system.

But how on earth is this happening? How could our Prime Minister be slowly making such a fundamental change to our tax system—shifting from taxing the individual to taxing couples—without anyone noticing and drawing it to our attention? Few people have noticed what Mr Howard's been up to because of the indirect and incremental means he's used and because he's never publicly admitted to it. But also because most of the experts who speak about tax matters are men—who either didn't notice or didn't consider it worth drawing attention to. The few female tax experts noticed it long ago, but no one's been listening to them.

So how has Mr Howard done it? By introducing his baby, the Family Tax Benefit, and then increasing its value at every opportunity. In fulfilment of an election promise, he introduced the benefit in his first, 1997 Budget, increased it as part of the GST tax reform package in 2000 and increased it again—by $600 a child—in the 2004 Budget. In the process he's lifted the value of the minimum benefit from about $600 a year per child to almost $1700 a year. The maximum benefit can be as high as $4900 per child.

The trick is that a family's eligibility for the benefit is subject to a means test, and the definition of income used is the couple's joint income. For a couple with dependent children, therefore, a big part of how much *net* tax they end up paying (that is, after allowing for what they get back through the Family Tax Benefit) turns not on their separate incomes but on their joint incomes.

Then, of course, there's the second part of the Family Tax Benefit, part B. Eligibility for part B—which is now worth up to $2900 a year per couple—is determined not by the couple's joint income, but solely by the wife's income. And the level at which the wife's income starts reducing her entitlement is so low that, in practice, part B turns out to be a special tax break for families where the wife doesn't work.

The point to note, however, is that if you're using the Family Tax Benefit as a backdoor way of equalising the net tax paid by single- and double-income couples with the same joint income, this must have the effect of raising the rate of tax being paid by working wives. Consider another of Professor Apps' examples. For 2003/04, a wife with a part-time job and an income of $20 000 a year would, if taxed as a single individual, pay less than $2700. Her average rate of tax would thus be 13.4 per cent. In fact, however, Professor Apps' estimate is that, on average, wives with part-time jobs earnt $19 200 a year and faced an effective average tax rate of 33.5 per cent. How come? Because, on top of paying income tax like any single person, the wives were penalised by the withdrawal of part of their Family Tax Benefit.

At a time when Treasurer Peter Costello wants as many people as possible to have paid employment and so help bear the cost of the ageing population, Australia's women don't have a high rate of participation in the labour force by international standards— particularly when you allow for the high proportion working only part-time. Why is our female participation rate low? One likely reason is that our Prime Minister thinks it a good idea to tax working mothers much more heavily than other people earning the same income. The other likely explanation is that, until recently, our Prime Minister also thought it a good idea to limit his government's spending on child care.

Let's turn to fertility. There doesn't seem much doubt that, along with the advent of the contraceptive pill in the mid-1960s, the marked decline in our total fertility rate—the number of children per woman—is linked to the rise in married women's participation in the workforce. From a peak of 3.6 in 1961, the fertility rate fell to 1.76 by the end of the 1990s—well below the population replacement rate of 2.1. Fortunately, the rate's been steady for the past six years. So maybe the further decline projected by the demographers won't eventuate. Sensible leaders, however, won't leave the matter to chance.

When he delivered the 2004 budget—which included the announcement of a new maternity payment—Mr Costello urged people to 'go home and do your patriotic duty'. His blokey humour may have been intended to cover up his marked change of tune on the question of fertility. When he released his Intergenerational Report in 2002, his line was that higher fertility would make the ageing problem worse and, in any case, there was little governments could do to influence it. It's true that, when the workforce is struggling to support more aged dependants, having more young dependants to support would make things harder.

But it's also pretty short-sighted. Though the community has to support young people for their first 20 or 25 years while they gain their education, thereafter they become workers helping to support others. As for Mr Costello's claim that governments can do little to influence fertility, it's simply not true—as his subsequent Budget and hilarious rhetoric now acknowledge. If you find it hard to believe the offer of a $3000—or, by 2008, even $5000—maternity payment could have much influence on couples' decisions to have children, you're right. Taken by itself, you'd expect the maternity payment's effect to be favourable, but tiny.

But such thinking views the issue too narrowly. The antidote is for all of us to absorb a surprising fact: those OECD countries with higher participation in the workforce by married women also tend to have higher fertility rates, whereas those countries with low female participation tend to have low fertility rates. That's about the opposite of what you'd expect, which is why we need to do a lot more thinking about the relationship between women, paid work and babies—not to mention husbands. (These insights come from the research of Peter McDonald, professor of demography at the Australian National University, and are confirmed by the research of Professor Apps.)

All the developed countries are experiencing rapid ageing of their populations, but most are a lot further down that road than we are. By the early 1980s, most European countries' fertility rates had fallen to about where ours is now. Some of those countries—Sweden, Norway, Denmark and France, for instance—responded to concerns about falling fertility by taking steps to make work more family-friendly. Others—Italy, Germany and Spain, for instance—didn't bother. Guess what? Those countries that have continued making life hard for working women have suffered both low rates of female participation and a continued fall in fertility, whereas the more enlightened countries have enjoyed both higher female participation and no further decline in fertility.

The key to this conundrum is to understand the implications of the revolution in women's levels of educational attainment. As we've seen, with girls being more highly educated than boys, it's no wonder so many of them want to enjoy the fruits of that education in terms of income and job satisfaction. And when, by the things they do or don't do, governments make it hard for women to have a career *and* a family, is it any wonder we end up with a lesser degree of workforce participation *and* declining fertility—not to mention a generation of mothers who aren't enjoying life as much as they should?

Frankly, I've come to the view that the men who dominate the policy-making in this area are really stuffing things up. Because they're oblivious to women's perspective, they're giving us too many mothers working part-time with too few kids when, if we knew what we were about, we could have more mothers working full-time with two or three kids. (What drove the fertility rate down was not so much the women deciding to have no kids as the mothers who settled for one or two rather than two or three.)

One reason we're not doing enough to make work more family-friendly is the ethic that says governments must do nothing that adds to the costs or inconvenience of the nation's employers. But the bad deal we're giving mothers (and the fathers, who should be doing more of the housework) is denying business full access to women's skilled labour, limiting the spending power of its customers and setting us up for a contracting domestic market. This is business people pursuing their self-interest? This is economic rationalists being rational? I don't think so.

One glaring area of policy neglect is child care. Adequate child-care facilities are vital to ensure the nation and its women gain full advantage from the huge investment in girls' education. Yet one of the Howard Government's first acts was to make the subsidy for paid child care less generous. All that changed—or seemed to—at the 2004 Federal election. Unfortunately, it's clear that while the government's spending on child care is now much more generous, it will do relatively little to increase the number of mothers able to participate in the labour force.

Included among the welter of expensive promises Mr Howard made in his election policy speech was the offer of a 30 per cent tax rebate on parents' out-of-pocket child-care expenses—that is, on the gap between fees paid for approved care and child-care benefit received. Although the promise was said to have a cost to other taxpayers of more than $1 billion over three years, little detail was given of how the concession would work. This may have involved deviousness, but it's more likely to have been because no one had thought that far ahead.

The child-care *rebate* was to be built on top of the existing child-care *benefit*—which most parents receive in the form of reduced weekly fees to their child-care provider. The value of the benefit varies between $3.05 and 47 cents an hour per child, depending on how many children are in care and the size of the family's combined income. I should tell you that, because of the memorable reaction to Mr Howard's unguarded remark about core and non-core promises after the 1996 election, Honest John's become a stickler for keeping 'em. But this doesn't preclude the Treasurer from doing a little retrospective redefinition of the terms and conditions of those promises. Sometimes this is to render the impractical practical; more commonly it's to make the promises less hugely expensive.

Either way, in this case Mr Costello and his Treasury advisers excelled themselves when it came time to implement the promise. The first newly revealed drawback of the child-care rebate was that, unlike the 30 per cent private health insurance rebate, people wouldn't be able to receive it in the form of reduced weekly fees through the year. Rather, they'd get it added to their tax refund cheque after they'd submitted their annual tax return.

But wait, there's more . . . Because the amount of your child-care rebate depends on the amount of your child-care benefit, because the amount of your child-care benefit depends on the amount of your family's combined income and your use of child care through the year, because these facts aren't known until after the end of the financial year, and because the bureaucrats can't work out the amount of your rebate entitlement until as late as November each year, you'll have to wait and claim your rebate in the *following* year's tax return. No, it's not a joke. It meant that, even though eligibility for the rebate was backdated to 1 July 2004, it would be more than 18 months from the day of that announcement before any parent saw a cent of it. And from then on, a rebate earned in (financial) year 1 wouldn't be received until early in year 3.

This belatedly revealed condition significantly reduces the rebate's practical value to all those families who struggle to afford the high cost of child care, particularly those where the wife's after-tax hourly wage rate doesn't compare all that well with the hourly cost of child care. In consequence, the rebate will do far less to encourage mothers back into the paid workforce than could have been expected. And compared with this catch, the six months' earlier starting date was hardly here nor there.

The second belatedly revealed drawback was that the size of rebates was to be capped at $4000 a year per child. This immediately restricted the value of the rebate to some mothers using highly expensive long day care in Sydney and Melbourne. For most other mothers it will be some years before they hit the ceiling. Even so, the cap will stop the rebate's cost to other taxpayers growing strongly year after year the way the cost of the 30 per cent private health insurance rebate has.

It's a matter of the simplest economics that when you use a 30 per cent subsidy to reduce the effective cost of something to the buyer, you increase the demand for it relative to supply and thereby permit the supplier to charge a higher price. In other words, the benefit of the rebate ends up being shared between the buyer and seller—as we've seen with the private health rebate. Mr Costello argued that the $4000 cap was intended to limit the scope for child-care suppliers (many of which are private businesses) to raise their prices—and, although he didn't say so, limit the scope for the woefully underpaid child-care workers to catch up with the rest of us. In practice, however, it's likely to be the extreme delay in people's receipt of their rebate that does more to inhibit suppliers in raising their prices.

Some critics of the rebate have argued that it will raise prices while doing nothing to improve the chronic undersupply of child-care places. That's wrong. To the extent that higher prices permit higher profits, in due course this will prompt suppliers to create more places. Trouble is, they're likely to be for-profit places aimed at highly paid mothers living in the better suburbs.

The government's newly acquired aim of making child care more affordable and available so as to encourage greater female participation in the workforce was laudable. Unfortunately, the bureaucrats' surreptitious efforts to knock the child-care rebate into shape didn't stop it being a relatively ineffective and wasteful way to pursue that goal. In our efforts to help couples balance work and family commitments, overcome the labour shortages arising from population ageing and at least halt the decline in fertility, we've still got a lot to fix.

It would be better to abandon the child-care rebate and use the saving to make the child-care benefit more generous. We could do more to encourage the establishment of community-provided child care in less prosperous suburbs where places are hard to find. And we really ought to summon up the courage to do what almost every other industrial country does and require employers to provide *paid* maternity leave.

CHAPTER 3
The cost of kids

It's heartening to remember that, although we live in a world of growing preoccupation with individualism and materialism, most of us still engage in the noble activity of raising children. It's the noblest thing we do. Raising kids is the main way that values such as loyalty, generosity, selflessness and caring are exercised by adults and developed in the next generation. It's the last bastion against the quid pro quo mentality of the market. There are emotional rewards for being a parent—as no one knows better than I do—and most of us hope it will bring us some joy in our old age. But, even so, it involves plenty of sacrifice.

Australia has 4.6 million children under 18, being brought up by about the same number of parents. Have you ever wondered how much it all costs? Or how good a job we're doing? Dr Sue Richardson, an economist at Flinders University in South

Australia, has. And she attempted to find out in her 2000 study, 'Society's Investment in Children'. It's a kind of cost-benefit analysis. It's a highly imperfect exercise, however—as she's the first to admit. We measure the things that are easy to measure—usually because they can have a dollar value attached to them—and tend to overlook the things that aren't, even though they're often more important.

But Dr Richardson does what she can, and leaves us better informed than we were. She starts with the obvious: how much parents have to shell out. Research confirms that the cost of children increases with their age and that subsequent children don't cost as much as the first—there are economies of scale. But the greatest variation in spending on children comes from the income of their parents. Estimates from the early 1990s show that the best-off 20 per cent of families spent on each child 2.6 times what the poorest 20 per cent of families spent.

Quite a difference, eh? But here's something I bet you don't know: most children live in high-income families. We're always being reminded of all the children living in poverty, but a third of the nation's children live in the 20 per cent of families with the highest gross family income. And two-thirds of them live in the top 40 per cent. Find that hard to believe? It's because the main way to have a high *family* income is not to be an obscenely overpaid executive, it's to have two income-earners. So most children live in high-income families because so many of their mothers are in paid employment. The typical child in a couple family has parents who, between them, work 40 to 60 hours a week.

The cost of kids

When you add it all up, you find that families spend about $720 million a week on their children, or $37 billion a year. But the mention of working mothers reminds us that, were it not for their children, most women would have working lives similar to men's. So their decision to have kids involves them forgoing a lot of income. They lose from their time out of the workforce, from the period in which they work part-time rather than full-time and from the opportunities for promotion this causes them to miss. Estimates by other economists have found that a woman's decision to have a first child reduces her earnings by an average of $6500 a year for the rest of her working life. Each additional child reduces her earnings by a further $4500 a year until the child reaches 16. Since the average mother has almost two children, her lifetime earnings are reduced by about $250 000. If you put that on the basis of what all mothers lose in any year, it works out at about $37 billion a year—which is on top of the $37 billion a year that all families spend on their kids.

But that's just the money parents give up. Next comes the time they give up. The Bureau of Statistics' survey of time use in 1992 shows that, between them, couples who have children spend about 140 minutes a day in direct child care as their main activity. This translates as about 2.5 million hours a year for all our children. And to this you can add about three times as much if you count the child care that takes place while parents are doing other things. Compare that with the 5.5 million hours a year that parents spend in their main paid job. But time spent on children is time not spent on other things. What other things? Mainly, sleep, watching television and free time.

Of course, it isn't just parents who bear the cost of children. Governments—and, through them, childless taxpayers—do too. Some of the money parents spend on children comes from the government in the form of the Family Tax Benefit and the Parenting Allowance, support which has grown markedly over the past 20 years. Total government spending on schools is at least $26 billion a year and spending on children's health and child care adds more. Put the whole shebang together and it works out to about 18 per cent of GDP.

But that's more than enough about costs—what about the benefits? How well are our kids doing as a result of all this expense? Here there are no answers to the most important questions. We know little about their emotional wellbeing or how happy they feel. So we fall back on the tangible measures. The vast majority are very well provided for. (This is not to deny the tragedy of those who aren't.) They live mostly in high-income families. Ninety per cent of them live in a separate house and only 4 per cent in a flat or unit. Only 4 per cent of their parents say they're dissatisfied with their housing.

Their health is very good. Australia's rate of infant mortality is among the lowest in the world and has fallen by a factor of 15 in the past century. Our children's rates of disability are low and their biggest health problem is asthma. They are generously fed, to the point where some are obese. Many should eat more fruit and vegetables and get more exercise. Despite increasing marriage breakdown, three-quarters of them live with both their natural parents and 94 per cent live with their birth mother.

For a minority, however, the story isn't good. Aboriginal children have worse outcomes on almost all these measures. For the whole nation, about 800000 children live in families where no parent is employed (almost 500000 of them in sole-parent families). At the other extreme, some families seem to be over-employed. The time-use figures show that some high-income couples devote little time to direct child care. And the direction of change in the workforce over the past decade has been to make it harder to combine parenting and paid employment. It's hard to believe that greater 'flexibility' in the labour market has worked to the advantage of parents, let alone their kids.

After that overview, let's look more closely at some specific aspects of child rearing, starting with all the time it takes up—a truth couples never fully understand until their first kid actually arrives. Intending parents should note the findings of a study by Dr Duncan Ironmonger, director of the Households Research Unit in the economics department of the University of Melbourne. 'Bringing up Betty and Bobby' came from Dr Ironmonger delving deep into the national time-use survey conducted by the Australian Statistician in 1992. The Statistician surveyed a sample of 3300 households across the nation, requiring the adults in each one to keep diaries of exactly how they spent their time for 48 hours.

If intending parents were to look at the published findings of the official survey they'd get a quite reassuring—but quite misleading—impression of the time kids take. They show that in 1992 the average Australian woman spent a mere 5.7 hours a week on child care, with the average man spending just 1.6 hours a week. By this reckoning, child care accounted for less than 16 per cent of the 37 hours a week of unpaid work that women did. In contrast, laundry and cleaning accounted for 24 per cent, meal preparation about 23 per cent and shopping about 18 per cent. For men, child care accounted for only 8 per cent of the 20 hours of unpaid work they did each week (little more than half what women did). Men devoted 20 per cent of that time to shopping, 17 per cent to gardening, 14 per cent to meal preparation and 11 per cent to repairs and maintenance.

But a moment's reflection reveals how misleading these figures are. For one thing, time spent on laundry, cleaning, meal preparation and even shopping is increased by the presence of children. More importantly, these figures are averages for *all* adult women and men (with 'adult' defined as 15 and above) and so include people who are either too young or too old to have kids that need to be cared for. You can see this when you look at the number of hours spent on child care by people of different ages. For females, teenagers spend about three hours a week (perhaps looking after their siblings) and women over 50 about two hours (perhaps looking after their grandkids). But the time spent by women hits a sharp peak of more than 16 hours a week in their early 30s. The pattern is similar—though the figures are a lot lower—for males.

Equally importantly, the figures are for time when child care is the *primary* activity—whereas, as every harassed parent knows, it *is* possible to do more than one thing at a time. (I suppose you could say the figures measure 'quality time'.) But if we stick to these imperfect figures for a moment, Dr Ironmonger reveals that—on a comparable basis—Australian women devote more time to child care than women in 11 other OECD countries. Australian men's performance is just above the international average, though well behind the gold-medal performance of Norwegian men (2.7 hours a week). So when you take men and women together, we get a silver after the Norwegians.

But, clearly, we need to delve deeper to give intending parents a more realistic picture. For a start, we need to take account of all the time that involves minding children while doing something else. When Dr Ironmonger does this he finds that the time *all* adults devote to child care quadruples. Time spent by women goes from 5.7 hours a week to 22.2 hours and time spent by men goes from 1.6 hours to 8.4. But we again need to narrow the focus to families that have kids. Dr Ironmonger does this by looking at only those households that have one child under 15.

This is where the hours pile up. It turns out that the average child in a single-child family gets 63 hours of care a week— provided mainly by the parents but, to a small extent, by other relatives and unpaid carers. But even this average is misleading because it conceals the fact that the amount of care children receive varies dramatically with their age. In the first two years of their lives, children receive 115 hours of (unpaid) care a week—which is almost 70 per cent of the number of hours there *are* in a week. In the following three years, they receive 77 hours of care a week. In the five years between turning 5 and turning 10, it drops to 66 hours and in the following five (until they turn 15) it drops to 30. (After that, it's not so much time the kids cost you as anguish.) To an economist's eye, the fact that the amount of time you have to devote to children falls so markedly as they grow suggests that investment in children involves rising returns over time.

But, needless to say, the care they get comes far more from women than men. This is particularly true in the first two years, when women provide 88 of the 115 hours of care. What I find interesting, however, is that the disparity diminishes somewhat as the kids get older. For kids aged between 5 and 9, for instance, the hours provided by women are 'merely' twice as great as those provided by men. If my experience is any guide, this may be because men think that, though babies are cute, kids are more interesting. I started taking more interest when at last I could have a decent conversation with my kids—or read them a 'chapter book', rather than *Sam Who Never Forgets* every night. And perhaps because, with boys particularly, fathers get involved with weekend sport.

Dr Ironmonger's calculations show that the amount of time devoted to children in single-child families exceeds the *average* amount of time devoted to all children by about 15 per cent. This is good news because it suggests there are economies of scale in the rearing of children. Subsequent kids don't require quite so much attention. But his study reveals some other truths which, though they'll come as no surprise to actual parents, may shock a few intendings.

One is that, once you take account of child care as a secondary way of using your time, a high proportion of reported child care occurs while the child's asleep. This, I suspect, is what does most to change your lifestyle. It restricts what else you can do and makes you more housebound. Another is that parents—presumably, those with babies—report that they're doing child care while they themselves are asleep. If you can't imagine how that could be possible, rest assured you'll find out (to coin a phrase).

The cost of kids

And Dr Ironmonger's research offers a further caution to those career couples who fondly imagine they'll solve their child-care problem by using paid care until their kid's old enough to have the problem solved by the school system. He finds that, of the 350 million waking hours of children under 15 in Australia in 1992, paid child care accounts for only 6 per cent of that time, and school for only 17 per cent. The kids look after themselves for about 20 per cent of the time, leaving parents and other household members to cope with the remaining 57 per cent. But don't let careworn parents deter you. The human species' survival thus far suggests that the benefits outweigh the costs.

Now let's take a closer look at a truth of which parents become painfully aware, but politicians prefer not to think about: kids get a lot more expensive as they get older. What follows is drawn from a survey of research evidence by the Australian Council of Social Service (ACOSS), 'Poverty, policy and the cost of raising teenagers'. Teenagers cost a fortune. For a start, they want a room of their own. Next are the gargantuan quantities of food they eat and the fancy clothes—and footwear—they insist on. Then there's the higher cost of their schooling and study. Last but by no means least is the big blighters' spending on 'recreation'—the $50 notes you have to shell out on Friday or Saturday nights, when they go out on the ran-tan while their oldies stay home with a book.

Research conducted in 1988 for the Department of Social Security, which developed a set of minimum budgets, estimated that it *should* cost $104 a week to look after a three-year-old (in today's dollars), but $162 a week for a 14-year-old. That's a 56 per cent increase. Another study, by researchers at the University of

Canberra, tried to estimate what families were *actually* spending. It found that the $375 a week they spend on 16- to 17-year-olds was four times what they spend on kids under five. We don't know how costs per child have changed over time. But we do have solid evidence to support another proposition parents well understand: with kids spending longer in education, they're leaving home later. (And when finally they do decamp, they're just as likely to come back.) We'll take a closer look at this in a moment.

So, while all this evidence has been amassing of the higher cost of older kids and the greater likelihood of them remaining dependent, have governments been adjusting family assistance to fit? No. In 1988 the Hawke Government introduced a higher rate of payment once kids turned 13, but that's all. Indeed, under the Howard Government it's been going the other way, as I discussed in the previous chapter. The whole Howard Government rhetoric about the need to 'find a better balance between work and family' essentially refers to reducing the indirect costs of children. And it's a completely legitimate cause for concern.

But think about this. Whereas the direct cost of kids increases as they get older, the indirect cost decreases. As the kids get a bit older, it's easier for mothers to return to paid work or to switch from part-time to full-time. And both parents will have advanced in their careers by the time their kids get into their teens. This means that, for middle-class two-income families, their time of greatest financial pressure is when their kids are very young. By the time the kids are older and costing a lot more, there'll be a lot more money about.

For less well-educated, jobless families, on the other hand, their time of greatest financial pressure is when their kids are

The cost of kids

oldest. This, of course, is the point the ACOSS study is making. Pretty much all the 'improvements' to family assistance payments in recent years have been directed at making the system more accommodating to the needs of middle-income earners. The notion that family payments are a key means of reducing child poverty has gone by the board.

(In fairness, however, I must acknowledge that, in all the benefits Mr Howard has delivered to his preferred single-income families, he's always cut sole parents in on the deal. Many sole parents don't have jobs, and many of their kids are in poverty.)

When I was helping pull together the book *How Australia Compares* a year or two back, I was dismayed to realise that Australia's record on child poverty is not one we can be proud of. According to a study done for UNICEF in 2000, out of 18 developed countries Australia came in 12th worst, with 12.6 per cent of our kids living in poverty. According to a more recent local study, it's nearer 15 per cent. Either way, nothing to write home about.

Finally, let's turn to a hidden consequence of Australia's push to become a Knowledge Economy. It's a wonderful thing, I'm sure. Our kids get more education and our workforce becomes more skilled than ever before. Girls are up there with boys, even surpassing them. But there's a hidden cost: much of the bill for our thirst for knowledge is falling on parents. As kids stay longer in education and join the workforce later, they're leaving the family home later and staying dependent longer.

And the changing demands of the labour market are being compounded by changes in government policy. Almost everywhere you turn, the forces of change are conspiring to add to the cost of supporting your offspring. It's not so much user pays as parents pay. According to official figures, almost half of all 20- to 24-year-olds still live with their parents. And even among those aged 25 to 34, 12 per cent still live at home. But the change sets in at a much earlier age, as shown by a research paper on the dependency of young people on their parents by Judy Schneider, then of the University of New South Wales's Social Policy Research Centre.

Dr Schneider found that, over the 14 years to 1996, the proportion of all 15- to 17-year-olds dependent on their parents rose from 79 per cent to 96 per cent. That was explained largely by the collapse in employers' demand for teenage full-time workers and the much increased number of kids staying on to Year 12 at school. Over the same period, the proportion of 15- to 17-year-olds with full-time jobs fell from 22 per cent to 8 per cent.

There's little reason to believe the story's changed much since then. About a third of young people go on to full-time university or other higher education—more than double the proportion in the early 1980s. This accounts for most, though not all, of the decline in the proportion of 18- to 20-year-olds in full-time employment which between 1982 and 1996 dropped from well over half to just over a third. Of course, most uni students have part-time jobs. That's what's happened to many of the former full-time jobs for juniors: they've been split up into part-time jobs and given to students.

But, despite their part-time employment, almost all the students in this age group remain dependent on their parents. (The study classed young people as dependent if their separate income was less than would be needed to keep them above the poverty line if they

The cost of kids

lived alone.) So the growth in university enrolments does most to explain why the proportion of all 18- to 20-year-olds dependent on their parents grew from less than 40 per cent in 1982 to more than 60 per cent in 1996.

Among older uni students—those aged 21 to 24—the story is more complicated. It seems that some of them now do sufficient part-time work to be able to support themselves. Since the mid-1980s, the proportion dependent on their parents actually fell—to a tick below 80 per cent! Even so, the proportion of *all* 21- to 24- year-olds who are still at uni rose over the years, so the proportion of *all* those in this age group still dependent stayed steady at 30 per cent.

Strictly speaking, to be still living at home is not necessarily to be still dependent on your parents. But the distinction is a blurry one. These days, the notion that kids who are earning should be paying board seems to have *gone* by the board. Where this happens, young people are still receiving some degree of support from their parents. (By the same token, to be living away from home is not necessarily to be completely free of financial support from parents.)

And don't assume—as many of us would—that the minority of young people who do have full-time jobs these days at least are freeing their parents of the need to support them. Far from it. According to Dr Schneider's findings, over the 14 years to 1996, the proportion of fully employed 15- to 17-year-olds who were nonetheless financially dependent on their parents rose from 10 per cent to two-thirds. The proportion of fully employed 18- to 20-year-olds remaining dependent rose to 16 per cent. Why?

Because junior wage rates—with 'junior' covering workers up to 21—fell in real terms, by 5 or 6 per cent over the 10 years to 1995. This is something to remember the next time you hear someone proposing lower junior wages as a solution to youth unemployment. Regardless of whether such a scheme would work, it would leave parents picking up the tab.

After that nasty twist, it's hardly necessary to add that there's been an increase in the proportion of unemployed young people who're dependent on their parents—though even in the early 1980s it was as high as 94 per cent. The youth dole has never been sufficient to let parents off the hook. So regardless of young people's status—whether they're in full-time education, full-time employment or are unemployed—the story's much the same: they've become increasingly dependent on their parents for financial support.

And while all these changes in education and the labour market have been digging deeper into parents' pockets, the government's been in for its chop, too. Under the rules of the 'youth allowance' that replaced the dole and Austudy in 1998, all payments to young people under 21 are now subject to a tight means test on their *parents'* income.

The government makes no bones about its reasons for engaging in such parsimony: it wishes to 'encourage families, to the extent they are able, to support their children until they have achieved financial independence'. Then, of course, there's the reintroduction of uni fees in the shape of HECS (discussed further in the next chapter). In principle, you can leave the fees as a debt to be paid off by your kids once they're out and earning.

The cost of kids

In practice, there's pressure on many parents to pay the fees up front (with the offer of a seemingly huge discount to add to the pressure).

For those of us who are doing well, all this evidence of the growing cost of getting the kids off your hands is just another thing to grumble about. After all, if you've got the dough, what more worthy cause to spend it on than your kids' upbringing? But it's not hard to see that, where families lack either the money or the willingness to support their kids for so much longer, it can lead to financial hardship and strained relations.

If raising children is the noblest thing we do, the world is conspiring to make it more noble than it was.

CHAPTER 4

The value of higher education

Having kids is a wonderful thing, of course, a privilege almost. But when it comes to educating them, our ambitions for their success give rise to some thorny—not to mention potentially expensive— decisions. While they're young, we make those decisions on their behalf. When they get older, *they* make the decisions—while we offer sage advice from the sidelines, with greater or lesser degrees of diplomacy and success. Because, these days, education and parental ambition tend to involve the outlay of large sums up front in pursuit of well-paid and successful careers for our offspring, it shouldn't surprise that economic researchers have advice to proffer.

Take the decision whether to send kids to a private school. If we're seeking social status—for ourselves as well as them—that's fine. In today's society, any conspicuous outlay of funds will help us along in the status race. But what if it's the inside running in the acquisition of a good degree we're seeking? Do private schools deliver the goods? And with such a high proportion of young people making it to uni these days, can we be confident a degree still makes sufficient difference to future earning power to justify the effort and expense? If *you* don't doubt it, your offspring might. Which brings us to the vexed question of HECS payments. Bearing in mind the hefty up-front discount, does the canny parent pay up front, or do they leave it for the kid to pay off once they find a job? Should the kid work longer hours to try to pay it off while at uni? Well, let's see what the presumed experts say.

In my observation of private schools, there's an unwritten contract between the parents and the school: we pay huge fees and, in return, you guarantee to get our kid to university. Question is: does it work? Well, if all you want is for your kid to make it to uni, it often does. But if you also want your kid to do well at uni, maybe not. Various studies have shown that, on average, students from private schools gain higher tertiary entrance ranks (TERs—now known as the universities admission index or UAI in New South Wales and the ENTER in Victoria) than students from government schools. According to one study, the average TER was 5.9 percentage points higher for independent schools and 5 percentage points higher for Catholic systemic schools.

But two recent studies by Paul Miller, professor of economics at the University of Western Australia (UWA), have put that result in a new light. One study, with Rosemary Win, looked at the academic performance of students completing first year at UWA. The other, with Elisa Rose Birch, looked at the performance of students completing first year at another, anonymous, large university.

Miller and Win found that, at the end of first year, the order of achievement had been reversed. Taking students with the same TER, those from government schools out-performed those from Catholic schools, with the Catholic kids out-performing those from independent schools. How is this reversal explained? Here, of course, we move from hard statistical fact to more arguable interpretation. Researchers argue that private school students tend to have higher TERs because they enjoy a higher level of confidence in their own ability, because the school environment is more conducive to learning and because their parents have higher aspirations for them.

It seems, however, that the superior resources and more attentive coaching of non-government schools serve to artificially inflate students' TERs relative to their raw abilities. The private schools' 'value-added' is short-lived. It may be that students from non-government schools have difficulty adjusting to the greater freedom and reduced supervision of university life. It's even been argued that some students from private schools are less enthusiastic because their courses have been selected by their parents.

You discover another reversal when you look at the types of school that students attended. Many studies have demonstrated that, in general, students do better in single-sex schools than co-educational schools. But Miller and Win found that students from co-ed schools tend to get better university grades than those from single-sex schools. Why? Perhaps because they're less flummoxed by getting to uni and discovering the opposite sex.

The value of higher education

Note that the two studies look at students' mark out of 100 at the end of first year, averaged over each subject studied. They therefore ignore those students who dropped out before the end of first year. Of course, not everyone who drops out is a drop-out. Some may have interrupted their study merely to spend some time travelling overseas. But those who fail to complete first year are more likely to be female, to be from rural areas and to have attended rural schools. They're also a bit more likely to have attended an independent school. The average TER of students who fail to complete first year, however, is only a little lower than that of those who do complete.

Many researchers have found that more highly educated and wealthier parents have children who, on average, perform better at school. Miller and Win confirmed that this carries through to university performance. It seems, however, that parents' level of education is more significant than their wealth. Research suggests that access to material things—such as nutritious food, comfortable housing and reading materials that stimulate intellectual interests—doesn't have consistent effects on children's learning. Rather, it's the skills of the mother—measured by the extent of her formal schooling—that are a critical factor in determining children's achievement.

You probably won't be surprised to hear that female students out-perform males in the first year of uni—on average, gaining grades more than 5 percentage points higher, according to Miller and Birch. What may surprise is that girls' superiority doesn't seem to be the case in other countries.

Miller and Birch found that, on average, students who've been accepted into courses that were only their third or fourth preference get grades 3.4 percentage points lower than those achieving their first or second preference. They're probably less motivated. They also found that students with a low TER, but who come from schools with a high proportion of kids going on to uni, tend to do better than expected in first year. They benefit from the 'immersion effect', where the university environment lifts them up. This is to be distinguished from the 'reinforcing effect', where students from schools that get good results in the tertiary entrance assessment tend to do better in first year than students from schools with poorer results.

Despite these various quirks, both studies confirmed that a student's TER is a good predictor of their success in first year. Miller and Birch estimated that each extra percentage point of TER is associated with an increase of between 0.75 and 1 percentage point in first-year grades.

But even this finding has a twist. All universities have arrangements that permit them to admit a small proportion of school-leavers with TERs below the official cut-off, but with special circumstances. Miller and Birch found that, on average, such students get first-year grades 7 percentage points higher than the grades of students above the cut-off. Special-admission students may be better motivated, but this finding also suggests that uni administrators can pick winners better when they judge applicants by factors other than just their TERs.

OK, after looking at these facts and figures, we've decided whether or not to patronise a private school and the hope of the side has made it to Year 12. Next question: why bother going to uni? With all the fees or debts they lumber you with these days

The value of higher education

under the euphemistically named Higher Education Contribution Scheme, is it still worth it? And what about the effect of the great surge in the numbers of school-leavers going on to uni in the past decade or so? Could it be that this increased supply of graduates has eroded the premium that people with degrees used to be paid in the labour market?

The research results are reassuring—up to a point. Though it's true that HECS is taking quite a bite out of the 'private return from university education', the monetary benefits remain significant. According to a study by Jeff Borland, professor of economics at Melbourne University, undertaken in 2002—admittedly, before the 25 per cent increase in HECS took effect in 2005—attending full-time university costs the average student more than $17 000 a year. Up-front HECS fees account for about $5000 of that, with such things as student union fees, books and travel costs adding a further $2000. So the greatest cost is the income students forgo by studying rather than working. Allowing for the many with part-time jobs, on average students are giving up about $10 000 a year in wages.

But here's the magic number that makes it all worthwhile (and is worth making a mental note of). According to Dr Borland's estimates, over the years university graduates earn an average of almost $10 000 a year more than high-school graduates do. And that's an *after-tax* figure. Putting it together, a three-year degree will have an initial cost averaging about $52 000, but lead to increased after-tax earnings over the graduate's working life of about $433 000, thus yielding a net total lifetime gain of about $380 000. (Note that, due to data limitations, these figures are for the average male graduate. You'd expect the lifetime gain to women to be lower—mainly because of fewer years in the full-time workforce and slower promotion.)

If you view the acquisition of a degree as though it was a business investment, it yields an average rate of return of 14.5 per cent a year. (This calculation is heavily influenced by the fact that all the costs are up front, whereas the benefits are spread over many subsequent years.) Now, if you know of many other investments that yield anything like as much as 14.5 per cent, please tell me. That's a good deal. But it remains true that, were it not for HECS, the rate of return would be 20.5 per cent.

So, roughly speaking (remember that all these estimates should be regarded as pretty rough and ready), we can say that HECS has reduced the private return on a university education by about a third. We can also say that the introduction of HECS seems to be the only factor that's reduced the return on uni education. Apart from that, the return's been quite stable for at least the past 20 years. So, though it's true the unis are churning out far more graduates than they used to, industry's demand for graduates seems to have grown in line with the increased supply, leaving graduate wage rates little affected.

It's worth noting that the figure of 14.5 per cent is the estimated return averaged over *all* three-year degrees. But you'd expect some degrees to lead to more lucrative occupations than others. Dr Borland's limited breakdown of the average confirms this. Arts and social science degrees, for instance, yield an average return of 11 per cent, whereas economics and business degrees yield 18 per cent.

The value of higher education

His estimates also show that, for those students who take four years to complete a three-year degree, the extra up-front cost cuts the rate of return from 14.5 per cent to 11.5 per cent or less. But what about the separate case of the return on an actual four-year degree—or on the increasingly popular double degrees, which can take five years or longer?

Dr Borland's study doesn't say it, but other research suggests that if you hang about unis for much longer than three years you soon encounter diminishing returns. It's probably right to expect that people who've done more years of study in their primary degrees will, on average, end up in better-paid jobs. But the extra income doesn't seem to be great enough to overcome the higher up-front cost caused by the delayed entry into the full-time workforce. And Dr Borland's study *is* clear on one thing: the rate of return on postgraduate degrees averages only 6.5 per cent—that is, roughly half what you get on a primary degree.

I can't let this topic drop, however, without reminding you of a point that I hope has been glaringly apparent to you. So far, my analysis of the benefits of tertiary education has been completely one-dimensional; it's focused solely on the monetary benefits. This is, unfortunately, a sign of our times. Economists, politicians, business people and the media have become increasingly obsessed by the economic role of education as a means of raising the productivity of labour.

This more materialist emphasis has prompted universities to make their courses more narrowly 'vocational' (not always a good move) and has seen students become much more mercenary in their attitudes. They show little interest in learning about anything that isn't examinable. And uni cultural activities are suffering as many students seek to improve their individual rate of return by devoting long hours to part-time work.

But you don't have to be a genius to see that education is worth pursuing in its own right, that it offers considerable intrinsic, non-pecuniary benefits. When we lose sight of those intrinsic benefits—knowledge for its own sake—we get muddled between means and ends. The irony is that when we allow ourselves to view higher education as little more than a better meal ticket, we impoverish ourselves.

Sorry, that slipped out. I was trying to stick to the strictly mercenary. And now let's take a strictly mercenary attitude to the question of the best way to pay HECS fees—up front or over time. People are terribly conscious of the 25 per cent increase in HECS applying to most (but not all) students starting uni in 2005 or later. A less publicised change—because it's good news—was the Howard Government's decision to raise the starting point for its repayment schedule from (in round figures) an annual income of $26 000 to one of $36 000. This change applies to all HECS payers, not just those affected by the 25 per cent increase.

The way the repayment schedule works is that how much you have to pay each year depends on how much you earn, and the more you earn the higher the percentage of your income you have to pay. It turns out that graduates earning less than $36 000 now make no repayments (a reduction in repayments of up to $1600 a year) and those earning between $36 000 and $54 000 now repay a couple of hundred dollars a year less, although those earning more than $54 000 now make faster repayments. Does that strike you as a significant concession to set beside the fee increase? It probably doesn't, but it should.

If you'll have to repay your HECS debt eventually, what's to be gained by postponing the evil hour? Ask all those business people who turn themselves inside out finding ways to defer paying their tax. Or try this: if you owed someone $1000 but they gave you the choice of paying today or in a year's time, which would you choose? That's obvious, but *why* would you delay making the repayment? Perhaps because it would allow you to avoid borrowing $1000 you needed for some other purpose. Or because, if you had the $1000 ready for repayment and had no other use for it, you could put it in the bank for a year and earn interest on it.

Of course, if you had to pay interest to the lender during the year in which you were delaying repayment, there'd be little to gain. But the thing people keep forgetting about HECS debt is that it carries no interest rate (though the principal outstanding is increased in line with inflation). So, with no *real* interest to pay, the longer you're given to repay your HECS debt, the less onerous it is. The more time you're given, the less interest you'll end up having to pay to other lenders, or the more interest you'll earn on your (higher) savings.

With an ordinary loan, the rate of repayment is set in concrete at the outset and doesn't vary if your circumstances change. But the other feature that marks HECS debt out from other loans is that the repayments are 'income related'. If you are unemployed for a period or you switch to working part-time, the repayments reduce to fit. So, though no one enjoys having to pay for their uni degree, the fact remains that a HECS debt comes on more generous and flexible terms than any other loan you'll get in your life.

Because the longer you get to repay your HECS the better off you are, students (as opposed to their doting and well-lined oldies) should think carefully before volunteering to repay their HECS earlier than required. If I've persuaded you that giving most people longer to repay their HECS gives them an advantage—a tangible benefit in terms of interest saved or interest earnt—the question then becomes how this benefit compares with the impost of the 25 per cent fee increase.

In a recent paper, Gillian Beer of the Natsem Centre at the University of Canberra, and Professor Bruce Chapman of the Australian National University—the inventor of HECS—did the (tricky) calculations to answer that question. They took the case of students starting uni in 2005 and compared what they would have had to repay over the years under the old rules with what they will have to pay under the new rules. But they took account of *when* repayments had to be made, not just how much they were. (For those who know the jargon, they applied a discount rate to the stream of payments to give the debt's 'present value'.)

They looked at HECS fees in the middle band—that is, more than for arts but less than for law or medicine—and assumed a four-year degree. If the increase in HECS was all there was to it then, obviously, the debt burden ought to be 25 per cent higher. But that turned out to be true—or almost true—only in the case of those students who ended up with earnings in the top third of all graduates' earnings.

For students who end up in the middle third of all graduates'

The value of higher education

earnings, the burden rose by 18 per cent for men and those women who had no children, but by only 9 per cent for women whose careers (and thus repayments) were interrupted by child-bearing.

Now get this: those students who end up in the bottom third of all graduates' earnings will actually be better off under the new deal. The males will be a fraction better off; the females will be a lot better off. Why? Because the benefit of having much longer to repay their loans—in some cases never fully repaying them—exceeded the cost of the 25 per cent fee increase. When you think carefully about HECS you discover it's not as bad as it sounds.

But that leaves the question of whether oldies should pay their kids' HECS up front, or leave it for the kids to pay off over time. Well, if the oldies are feeling munificent, sure. But if they're motivated by a desire to take advantage of the big up-front discount the government offers, then no. As we've seen, HECS debt constitutes a real-interest-free loan. That's a valuable concession (given that you're lumbered with having to pay HECS whichever way you jump) and the longer you're given to repay the debt the more valuable the concession. The concession is so valuable it's highly unlikely the up-front discount would be worth more. That was true when the discount was 25 per cent; it's even truer now it's been cut to 20 per cent.

If you find that reasoning a bit hard to follow—or far too cold-heartedly calculating—let me tell you, if you go to uni to do an economics, commerce or business degree, that's just the way they teach you to think.

CHAPTER 5
The Great Australian Home

Whoever decided that an Englishman's home is his castle had obviously never met an Australian. When it comes to being obsessed with housing, Aussies can give the Poms and anyone else a run for their money. But that's not so much because of The Great Australian Dream of wanting to own the home we live in. While it's true that about 70 per cent of our homes are owned by their occupants—with half of those being owned outright—there's been little change in that 70 per cent since the 1970s. In the meantime, most other English-speaking countries have caught up or even passed us. In 2000, our rate of home ownership was about the same as in Britain and Canada, and only a bit higher than in the United States, but lower than in New Zealand and newly prosperous Ireland—the winner at 83 per cent. The Italians beat us, too.

The Great Australian Home

For proof of Australians' obsession with our homes we need to look further afield than mere ownership. Consider first the remarkable growth in the size and quality of our homes. According to Clive Hamilton and Richard Denniss in *Affluenza*, between 1985 and 2000 the average floor area of new houses increased by almost a third, from 170 square metres to 221 square metres, and the size of apartments increased by a quarter to an average of 139 square metres. In the mid-1950s, the average size of a new house was half the size of a new house today. Many new homes now have three-car garages.

'This expansion in the size of houses has been occurring at a time when the average number of people in each household is shrinking', Hamilton and Denniss write. 'In 1955 each household had an average of 3.6 people . . . and by 2000 it had reached only 2.6 people. Put another way, in 1970 an average new house had 40 square metres of floor space for each occupant, whereas today each occupant has 85 square metres.' But while the houses have been getting bigger, the blocks of land they're sitting on haven't. So backyards have been shrinking—with the result, presumably, that today's kids spend a lot more time indoors.

How have we been able to afford this continuing increase in quantity and quality? Well, our material standard of living has improved by about 90 per cent since 1970. As well, there's our willingness to devote an increasing proportion of our incomes to housing. But let me mention one little-recognised factor: the rise in the *price* of homes and the amount we spend on them is partly an unintended consequence of the rise of the two-income household. When the first couples decided it would be a good idea for the wife to take paid employment, this gave them a considerable advantage in the housing status race. Their combined incomes allowed them to afford the repayments on a much bigger and better house than other couples. But once most other couples joined in, the advantage was lost. The main effect of two-income couples' greater purchasing power was to force up the prices of the sorts of houses couples buy. Now, couples who want to keep up with the Joneses have less choice about whether the wife takes paid employment.

But the most remarkable evidence of our preoccupation with housing is the seven-year property boom to the end of 2003, in which the price of houses more than doubled. The size and length of that boom is explained overwhelmingly by one development: our return to low inflation, which over time brought about a halving in mortgage interest rates. According to the standard formula the banks use to determine how much they're prepared to lend to a borrower, a halving of interest rates roughly doubles the amount you can borrow. But let's not jump to conclusions. When you think about it you realise there were three possible responses to the steady decline in mortgage interest rates during the 1990s.

First, people could have left their monthly repayments unchanged, knowing this would mean they'd be debt free a lot earlier than expected. Second, they could have had their monthly repayments cut to the minimum permitted, thus giving themselves a lot more cash to spend on other things. Or third, they could have traded up to a much more expensive home without any great increase in their monthly repayments. Though plenty of people did each of these things it's clear that, in the main, they traded up.

The Great Australian Home

Why was this the way most people chose to jump? It seems pretty clear we were responding to a long-standing unfulfilled demand for higher-quality housing. We'd always wanted to spend more on housing, but couldn't afford to. So as soon as the cost of borrowing fell we leapt in. Now, you'd expect the halving in interest rates to be an absolute boon for first-home buyers. Young couples—and not-so-young couples—who formerly hadn't been within cooee of affording to buy a home would now have their big chance to enter the market.

But research by the Reserve Bank shows it didn't work out like that. The proportion of housing finance going to first-home buyers has been, taken over the full seven years of the boom, little different from normal. So the huge increase in demand for housing—and housing finance—didn't represent a huge increase in the number of home owners. Rather, the existing home owners elbowed aside a lot of potential first-home buyers in their rush to improve their position in the market.

The final pointer to our obsession with housing comes from a particular feature of the boom: the special role played by investment housing. We used to worry we might become a nation of renters, but now we've become a nation of landlords. No more gambling on the stock exchange—good old bricks and mortar have triumphed as the dinkum Aussie's investment of choice. It seems a lot of baby boomers and others realised they hadn't saved enough towards their retirement and so got into investment property as a way of catching up in a hurry.

Of all the new money the banks and others were lending for housing, the proportion going to investors rather than owner-occupiers reached 40 per cent. And of all the money we owe on housing, no less than a third is owed on rental properties. That's up from just 15 per cent at the start of the 1990s. Only about a third of households have mortgages.

But get this: the proportion of households owning investment properties has now reached 17 per cent. Among the richest 20 per cent of households, it's about a quarter. This preoccupation with bricks and mortar is very Australian. In the United States and Canada, the proportion of households with property investments is less than half what it is here. In Britain it's just 2 per cent.

According to the Reserve Bank, 'in earlier decades, investment in rental property was an option only for the well-off and well-connected because of the difficulty in obtaining finance'. But that's changed. These days the banks fall over themselves to offer you investment loans. In the old days, people wanting to borrow for investment paid an interest rate 1 percentage point higher than owner-occupiers. That's gone. In other English-speaking countries, the banks still aren't so keen to lend to landlords.

And in other countries, investors in rental property don't get the tax breaks they get here. We give property investors a full tax deduction for their interest payments and any other expenses—no questions asked—plus deductions for depreciation of the building and its fittings. When we make a capital gain, we tax it at half rates. In its submission to the Productivity Commission's inquiry into first-home ownership, the Reserve Bank quoted an example of someone buying a $400 000 rental apartment and borrowing all the price. Because the interest payments far exceed the rent received, the landlord was out of pocket to the tune of $330 a

The Great Australian Home

week. But that was before tax. Allow for all the tax breaks and it reduced to $80 a week.

Then there was the ubiquitous 'investment seminar', in which the sure-fire money-making magic of rental property was explained to unsophisticated investors—and which seems to have been an Australian invention. The infamous 'deposit bond'— which allowed you to buy an apartment 'off the plan' with an initial outlay of just $1000 or $2000—was also an Australian invention.

There was just one small problem: the number of people wanting to be landlords got out of whack with the number wanting to be tenants. We built more rental accommodation than we needed. That was evident in falling apartment prices, particularly in Sydney and Melbourne. And the return on residential property investment was and is pathetic. The yield—rent received as percentage of the market value of the property—used to exceed 8 per cent in the mid-1980s, but fell to about 3.5 per cent (and 2.5 per cent when you allow for expenses such as rates, maintenance and agent's fees). For commercial property (factories, shops and offices) it's still about 9 per cent. And it's 8 per cent or better in Britain and North America. Our very low yields were a sign of the tail wagging the dog, of landlords being keener to supply than tenants were to demand.

Returning to the main game, it's clear the boom was led by existing home owners. Fuelled by the increased purchasing power the fall in interest rates had delivered them, they wanted to trade up to better homes. So whereas the surge in demand from investors represented a demand for *more* homes (particularly apartments), the demand from existing home owners was for *better* homes. Better in what respect? For some people that meant bigger or better-appointed homes, but I think for most it meant better-located homes—homes in more highly regarded parts of the city. Sometimes 'location, location' means suburbs closer to the harbour or the beach, but I think these days it more often means 'proximity, proximity'. The big long-term trend in real estate is that people want to live closer to the centre of the city—although harbour/beach and closer in aren't necessarily mutually exclusive.

The great desire to live closer in explains the rash of newly built apartments in or near the CBD. Even so, the supply of well-appointed *houses* in well-regarded, close-in suburbs is reasonably fixed. See the point? What happens when a whole bunch of existing owners enjoy a huge increase in their borrowing—and therefore purchasing—power at pretty much the same time and start fighting over a reasonably fixed supply of well-appointed and well-located homes? The price of homes is bid up a long way.

More than doubled, in fact. Between June 1996 and December 2003, the median house price in Sydney rose by 130 per cent, in Melbourne by 140 and in Brisbane by 120 per cent. It's worth remembering, however, that Sydney prices were more than 40 per cent higher than Melbourne prices before the boom started. So whereas the *national average* median house price was 6.6 times average annual earnings in December 2003, and the Melbourne median was 7.6 times, the Sydney median was almost 10 times annual earnings.

There was a bit more to the boom than that, however. The

The Great Australian Home

property market, of course, is notorious for moving in cycles of boom and bust. Why? Mainly, I suspect, because humans are herd animals. When we see other people trading up to better homes, we have an almost irresistible urge to join them. We have a fear of being left behind as the herd moves on. With property, of course, we see prices shooting up and convince ourselves that, if we don't get in quick, we'll have lost our chance. These expectations of perpetually rising prices are self-fulfilling and self-perpetuating—for a time. But for reasons that, in each specific case, are rarely very clear, booms always come to a stop—often with a bang but sometimes, fortunately, with a whimper.

So while at one level this boom represented a once-only adjustment to the return to low inflation and interest rates, as well as a continuing shift in home owners' preferences to be 'closer in', at another level the rise in prices is likely to have been overdone—particularly because of the contribution to the frenzy of the tax-driven and highly speculative surge in borrowing for property investment.

The boom's well and truly over by now, of course, so where does it leave us? Judging by the Howard Government's thumping re-election in October 2004, most of us are well pleased. Nothing like soaring house prices to make voters happy. In truth, however, we're not as well off as many people assume. A lot of people think that if there's one thing about the economy they do know something about, it's real estate. But there's a lot of illusion associated with the property market.

The first example is one of perspective. From the viewpoint of the individual, house prices soared in the late 1990s and early 2000s and there wasn't anything you could do about it. If you wanted to move to a better home you just had to borrow vastly more than you would have a few years earlier. That's true for every individual. And yet it's also highly misleading. Why did house prices rise? Was it the government that put them up, or the dastardly real estate agents? Hardly. They rose as a consequence of the concerted actions of all those powerless individuals. They all started bidding for a relatively fixed stock of established houses at pretty much the same time. They all had the ability to borrow more and the willingness to do so, with the result that prices were bid up.

The second example of illusion is political. John Howard and his ministers are always reminding us of how much better off we are since they got interest rates down. It's certainly true that mortgage interest rates are a lot lower today—around 7 per cent—compared with what they were under the Labor Government—the peak of 17 per cent in 1989 or even the 10.5 per cent they were when Mr Howard took over in March 1996. But if the main consequence of the fall in rates has been to allow us to bid up the prices of homes—thus requiring individuals to borrow sums at least twice as large as before—how exactly are home-buyers better off? When rates were at 17 per cent, households' interest payments averaged about 9 per cent of their disposable income. When Labor lost office in 1996, it was 7 per cent. These days it's nearer 11 per cent.

The third case of illusion is actually one of the lesser-known conclusions of economics: that a doubling in the value of our homes doesn't really make us any wealthier. Find that hard to swallow? Well, let's think about it. As we've seen, the greatest single cause of the boom was the halving of mortgage interest rates over the course of the 1990s, which permitted everyone to borrow more for housing. Some new homes were added to the existing stock and other people renovated. Some first-home buyers were able to take advantage of the lower rates but, for the most part, the boom consisted of a lot of existing home owners buying other people's existing homes. And remember that existing homes outnumber new homes by roughly 50 to one.

So the housing boom boiled down to a ginormous game of musical chairs. All these people moving on to homes they considered to be bigger, better built or better located. But apart from all the moving around, the main thing this does is bid up prices. So, between us, we've taken a largely unchanged stock of homes and doubled the price of it. Question is, how does that make us wealthier?

Say you've been sitting tight, watching the value of your home soar. How are you better off? The main thing that's changed is your rates are higher. If you decide to sell and move to a better place, it's a safe bet the price of that place has been rising at pretty much the same rate as your place has. And if its price started out higher than yours, the price gap you must borrow to cover is now bigger in dollar terms.

If, on the other hand, you decide to trade down to a smaller or cheaper place, you can expect to walk away from the trade with money in your hand (though of course the price of the place you're moving to has also been rising). So you can really only capitalise on the property boom if you were an owner before the music started and you're now prepared to scale down your home or move out of the city to a cheaper town.

You see from this how property booms are biased in favour of the old and against the young. And that's a reminder of a further reason home owners with children (or grandchildren) may doubt that they're better off. How will your kids afford a home at these exorbitant prices? They won't—not without your help. And if you've got one home but two or three kids who'll need a lot of help with their deposit, why should you be so chuffed about the doubling in house prices?

To an economist, the significant thing about owner-occupied housing is that it's a consumption good as well as an asset. That is, we need somewhere to live and we live in our homes. If you were to capture the capital gain on your home by selling it, you'd have to rent. But rents are expected to fully reflect the value of the place you're renting. So you're better off because of the capital gain, but worse off because you now face a lifetime of rent payments that are higher than they would have been without the boom. Thus while some individuals gain from a property boom and others lose, the community as a whole is no wealthier in a real sense.

But let's take a closer look at the situation from an inter-generational perspective. Young people are entitled to look at today's house prices and wonder how on earth they'll ever afford a home of their own. On the other hand, we know the parents of the baby boomers will be the first generation to die leaving hefty inheritances to their children—largely because of the huge appreciation in the value of their homes, not just over the past decade but over the past 30 years or more. We know, too, that as well as these inheritances, the home-owning baby boomers have done well out of their own homes.

The Great Australian Home

But there are the baby boomers' kids, priced out of the property market. You could understand if they were starting to feel it was all terribly unfair. Fortunately, it's not as bleak as it looks. Fallback No. 1 is the one I've already alluded to: the milk of familial kindness. The instinct to see your kids right is a strong one, and I think it will soon be common to see parents coughing up deposits, going guarantor for their offsprings' loans, taking on part of the loan themselves and otherwise making sure their kids get a toehold on the ladder of home ownership. Our ever-helpful banks are already promoting 'products' that facilitate such arrangements. Nor will I be surprised to see some grandparents bypassing their children and leaving money to their landless grandkids.

What of all the talk of the improvident boomers, however? You often hear it suggested that they haven't saved enough to permit themselves to live in retirement in the comfortable style to which a lifetime of self-indulgence has made them accustomed. What if, rather than 'recycling' the value of their homes to their children, they take the sea-change or tree-change option, selling their city homes, moving to a cheaper town and using the difference to bolster their retirement income? If the baby boomers consume their own wealth, where does that leave their kids? Well, that's where any lack in the milk of familial kindness is countered by the iron laws of economics.

Two points. A house is worth what you believe it's worth only if you can find a buyer willing and able to stump up that amount. It is, in fact, worth not a cent more than you can sell it for. And broadly speaking, this generation sells its homes to the next. So if the rising generation can't afford the prices the previous generation believes their homes to be worth, guess what? The prices come down until the next generation *can* afford them. So to the extent the baby boomers are too absorbed with their own problems to help out their children, market forces will take their supposed wealth from them and give it to their kids in the form of lower prices.

And don't be sceptical. It's already happening. House prices peaked in the December quarter of 2003. Over the following two years, they rose by less than 3 per cent in Melbourne—below the inflation rate of 5 per cent—and fell by more than 8 per cent in Sydney. So house prices are weakest in those cities where they reached the dizziest heights. And Sydney prices have returned to being just 50 per cent higher than the average for the other capital cities, where they were before the boom started. Just how long the period of house prices being 'flat to down' persists is anyone's guess. But precedent suggests it could persist for some years yet. According to figures from the Real Estate Institute of Australia, in the two years following the (much smaller) boom of the late 1980s, the median house price in Sydney fell by 25 per cent.

One important difference with this boom is that, unlike all its predecessors, it died of old age rather than being choked off by a sharp rise in interest rates. As a result, it ended more with a whimper than a bang. That's relatively good news for the housing market and the wider economy. Sharp rises in interest rates usually lead to recessions. The consequence, however, may be a period of weakness in house prices that's more protracted than usual.

When housing booms reach their peak, people are always concerned that house prices have become unaffordable for first-home buyers. More experienced observers know not to worry. Why not? Because markets always correct—they have to. One way or another, quickly or slowly, prices have to fall to levels most buyers are able to afford.

CHAPTER 6
Saving, debt and guilt

Human nature is a trickier thing than we imagine and even the mundane activities of our daily lives are more complex than we realise. For one thing, we seem to be subject to some kind of compensatory mechanism that prevents us feeling we've attained the goals we strive for. Most of us, for instance, would like to feel 'financially comfortable'—to have a bit more income than we need to make ends meet. To have some savings put by. And, since Australians' real income per person has risen by more than half in the past 20 years, you'd expect most of us would finally have attained that goal. According to opinion polls, however, almost two-thirds of Australians believe they can't afford to buy everything they really need.

How could that be so? Well, I think it happens because most of us think money is for buying things and most of us have an infinite list of things we'd like to buy if only we had the dough. So, every time we get a pay rise, we lose little time in spending it, taking on the extra commitments that are now possible. It follows that, no matter how high our pay has risen in the past or may rise in the future, we'll always be fully committed. We'll always feel that we're just making ends meet, with nothing to spare.

It also follows that our vague ambition to put something by has lost out to our much stronger urge to buy more stuff. That battle's continued for decades, and spending has now triumphed over saving. The first half of the noughties will be remembered as the time when Australians finally gave up the practice of saving. But I have a feeling it won't be a milestone we look back on with any joy. Consider this. In 1975, the nation's households saved 16 per cent of their after-tax income. Today, they're saving minus 3 per cent. That is, households' consumer spending is 3 per cent *more* than their after-tax income.

It seems saving has simply gone out of fashion. As Clive Hamilton and Richard Denniss observe in their book *Affluenza*, in the modern world—and by some kind of financial alchemy—'saving' has become something we do while we're spending. Bargain hunters can easily 'save' hundreds of dollars in the mid-year sales. Choose what you buy carefully and the more you spend, the more you save.

The abandonment of (genuine) saving is all the more surprising when you remember how many baby boomers are approaching retirement. But here, too, financial alchemy is in evidence. How often have you heard boomers explaining that they bought a negatively geared property investment as a way of saving for retirement? So these days, 'saving' involves borrowing almost all the money needed to buy a property, then hoping to clean up through capital gain.

The two great middle-class virtues have long been the belief in the value of education and the belief in the value of saving. What they have in common is an acceptance of delayed gratification. Both require the exercise of self-discipline. And in this we gain a clue to what's changed. Economists define saving as 'deferred consumption'; in other words, you can only save more by consuming less (which is the hard part). Saving and borrowing are, of course, opposite sides of the same coin. We save when we spend less than all our income on consumption. How can we have our consumer spending *exceed* our income? By borrowing the difference (or running down past savings).

What's changed—and what's led us to go from being positive savers to negative savers—is the greater ability for people of ordinary means to borrow freely and relatively cheaply. One key change was the advent of credit cards. Credit cards reached Australia in the mid-1970s with the unsolicited distribution of Bankcards. Over the past decade or so, however, the banks have been really pushing credit cards. So much so that the total amount we owe on our cards has more than sextupled in the past 12 years to reach $34 billion. (More about credit cards a bit later.)

A more recent innovation is the highly advertised 'home-equity' loan. Any home owner with a fair bit of equity can now borrow—for any purpose—simply by increasing the size of their mortgage. And do so at the mortgage interest rate, which is far cheaper than borrowing through a credit card or personal loan. Historically, home owners have been keen to pay off their mortgages ASAP, increasing their equity. Home-equity loans put paid to that and we've just been through our first-ever period of declining equity.

The third thing that's changed is the attitude of the banks. Where once you had to beg them to lend to a mere mortal such as yourself, now they're thrusting loans on you. In consequence, the past 12 years have seen a blow-out in personal debt—including credit cards, personal loans, car loans, etc.—from $40 billion to $120 billion.

Allied with the greater availability of credit is, I suspect, another factor: our increasing disconnectedness from money. Money has become more a concept—a book entry on your bank statement—and less a bunch of banknotes in your wallet. These days, the money still passes through our hands, but we don't see it as clearly. We get paid by a direct credit to our bank account and increasingly we pay for things with plastic. Credit cards foster the illusion that we can buy things without having to pay for them. We all know it's an illusion, of course, but I doubt if it's only a few innocent teenagers who fall for it.

We curse the banks, but it hasn't stopped us becoming hugely more indebted to them. The spread of consumer credit is assumed by economists to be one of the great boons of the late capitalist period. No longer being 'credit-constrained' is meant to allow us to spread our consumption more evenly over our life cycle; instead, it's allowed us merely to indulge our impatience to buy the latest electronic gadget and made us more susceptible to the lure of advertising.

It's important to recognise that not all debt is bad. Borrowing to buy your home makes much sense because you're buying an asset that should at least retain its value, as well as eliminating the need to pay rent. It's borrowing for consumption that's more questionable.

We used to have to save up before we could buy things, now we don't. As Hamilton and Denniss point out, we've gone from pre-saving to post-saving—buying something on credit, then paying it off over time. Trouble is, you can only make that shift once. And just as under the old rules you couldn't buy something before you'd saved the money, under the new rules you can't buy the next thing until you've paid off the last one—with interest.

Consider this example from Hamilton and Denniss: anyone who racks up $5000 of debt during 2006 will need to reduce their consumption expenditure by more than $11 000 in 2007 if they want to get back to where they were. Blow your credit card out by $5000 and there are three separate hits to your lifestyle. First, you can't keep spending $5000 more than you earn, so you'll have to cut back your spending—by about $100 a week—just to avoid getting further into debt. Second, you have to repay the $5000, which will require a cut in your spending of a *further* $100 a week. Third, you'll also have to pay interest which, at a rate up to 18 per cent, is likely to add up to more than $1000. (No wonder so many of the people who play these games feel they're having trouble making ends meet.)

Interest. That's the rub. We can get our hands on something earlier, but the interest we have to pay on the borrowed money is the price of our impatience. There's no free lunch in the new world of freely available credit. With so many people adding to their mortgages (so that the stuff they buy is paid off only over the next 20 years or so) or running a permanent balance of several thousand on their credit card (at piddling interest rates of up to 18 per cent), just think how much money we're losing in interest.

You may think it's the poor who tend to borrow rather than save, since the rich don't need to, but that's a misperception. Though it's true the advent of credit cards has given people on modest incomes much more ready access to credit at less than usurious interest rates—allowing them to escape the clutches of pawnbrokers and loan sharks—it's also true the banks prefer to lend to people who don't need it. They're always more comfortable lending to people with 'collateral'—assets that can be linked to the loan and used to repay it if the worst comes to the worst. This explains why the banks are pushing home-equity loans with such vigour (and why increasingly they require small business people to use their homes as security for business loans).

A study by the Reserve Bank using figures from 2002 found that, of the two-thirds of Australian households with some form of debt, the 30 per cent with the highest incomes accounted for almost 60 per cent of the total debt outstanding. By contrast, the 40 per cent with the lowest incomes accounted for just 14 per cent. This distribution reflects both a higher proportion of high-income households with debts and the higher average size of those debts. It's clear, too, that the recent surge in negatively geared property investment is concentrated among the better-off. The top 30 per cent of households with debt accounts for three-quarters of the total investment-property debt, whereas the bottom 40 per cent accounts for less than a tenth of it.

Another small fact that may surprise: people in rich countries tend to save a much lower proportion of their incomes than people in poor countries. That's particularly true of the English-speaking developed countries, whose householders tend to be the worst savers in the world. Australian households have a negative rate of saving, as we've seen, and American households aren't much better. But China's households save 16 per cent of their income, while India's save 24 per cent.

Why do people in poor countries save so much more than we do? Because people need a motive to save, and people in poor countries have plenty—to pay for their kids' education; in case they get sick and have big hospital bills as well as being unable to work; in case they lose their job and can't find another; and for the time when they're too old to work. Get it? In rich countries we have laws and government benefits to cover all those contingencies: free public education, Medicare, paid sick leave, the dole and the age pension. In other words, in setting up the welfare state so as to greatly diminish the risk of our falling into extreme financial hardship, one of the unintended consequences has been to greatly diminish our motive to save. There's nothing new about the welfare state, of course—it's been with us for at least 60 years. But combine it with the more ready availability of reasonably priced credit and our will to save seems to have evaporated in the face of all the temptations presented by a hyper-consumerist economy.

I must add, however, that just because you and I are saving little on our own account doesn't mean other institutions aren't saving on our behalf. For one thing, the budget surpluses govern-

Saving, debt and guilt

ments tend to run these days represent saving on their part—raising more through taxes than they need to cover their recurrent spending. For another, companies save when they retain part of their profits rather than paying them all out in dividends to shareholders. And companies are retaining more of their earnings than they used to. The consequence is that, despite the decline in saving by households, the *nation*—representing households, governments and companies—is saving about as much as usual.

So far I've avoided saying too much about borrowing for housing, believing it's a lot easier to justify. It provides a roof over your head and relieves you of the need to pay rent, not to mention the possibility of capital gain. But it can't be ignored if you want the full story about the growth in household debt. In January 2006, Australia's households had total debt of $850 billion. This was up by a factor of five on what it was just 12 years earlier. But note this: borrowing for housing accounted for 86 per cent of the total households owed. And borrowing for housing accounted for an even higher proportion of the *growth* in the total that households owed, notwithstanding the figures I quoted earlier for the dramatic growth in non-housing 'personal' debt.

It's common to compare the amount households owe with their annual disposable income. Twelve years ago, Australian households had borrowed the equivalent of about 60 per cent of their annual income—which was low by the standards of other developed countries, including the United States and Britain. Today, however, our debts have risen to more than 150 per cent of our annual income—which is among the highest in the developed world. Gosh.

Fortunately, however, when you think about that startling statistic you realise it's not as bad as it sounds. For a start, as we've seen, almost all the growth in debt has come from borrowing for housing. So while households' debts have grown enormously, so too have the value of their assets. Were the worst to come to the worst and some home buyers find themselves unable to keep up the payments on their mortgage, most would be able to use the proceeds of the sale of their home to clear their debts and get on with the rest of their lives. For the vast majority of owner-occupiers, however, it's most unlikely to come to that.

I suspect it's the fact the ratio has pushed above 100 per cent that makes it sound so shocking. But think about it. Why is the amount of your annual salary a relevant comparison to the amount you've borrowed? It isn't. Whoever imagines you could buy a house and have it paid off within the first twelve months? That's why home-loan contracts typically run for 20 or 25 years—to give you plenty of time to pay off such a huge sum. And whoever had to borrow no more than their annual salary to reach the price of their home? Didn't you? It's perfectly normal for people to borrow three or four times their annual salary. And if that doesn't bother the borrowers—or the banks that did the lending— why should it worry you and me?

Actually, if the typical new home loan is three or four times the borrower's salary, it makes you wonder why the ratio isn't even higher than 150 per cent. It's because almost a third of Australia's 7.7 million households are renting, and so have no housing debt, while more than a third own their homes outright, leaving only a third with mortgages. What's more, a fair few of those would have had their mortgages for many years and so be well advanced in paying them down. When we think of home-buyers we tend to think of struggling young couples taking on big mortgages to bridge the deposit gap, but they're the minority. As we've seen, the majority of household debt is owed by people who are quite comfortably off.

But if comparing households' debt with their annual disposable income doesn't make a lot of sense, how should we assess the ability of households to manage their debt? By looking at the proportion of their disposable income they must devote to the interest and principal repayments on their debt. In 1989, when mortgage interest rates were at their all-time peak of 17 per cent, households' interest payments accounted for a bit over 8 per cent of their disposable income. (You could add another couple of percentage points to that for repayments of principal.) Today, with mortgage rates down around 7 per cent, interest payments account for a new record of about 11 per cent. Why so much higher when interest rates are so much lower? Because the doubling of house prices has greatly increased the *amounts* people have borrowed, countering the advantage of the lower rates.

But if 11 per cent doesn't seem high, remember that two-thirds of households have no debt on their homes. Returning to the Reserve Bank's study of the commitments of those households that did have owner-occupier housing debt in 2002, we find that those in the upper income bracket used, on average, less than 20 per cent of their after-tax income to meet interest and principal repayments. The comparable figure for lower-income households was about a third of after-tax income. That's a lot higher than 11 per cent, but it's not too bad. And note, too, that more than half of home-buying households were ahead of schedule on their debt repayments, giving them a bit of leeway should times get tough.

Of course, to say that most home-buyers seem to be on top of their mortgage payments and could survive a rise in interest rates unscathed is not to say they all could. A further breakdown of the figures reveals that about an eighth of those households with incomes in the second-lowest quintile (20 per cent grouping) have mortgages and, of these, 18 per cent have repayments equivalent to more than half their after-tax incomes. Although they represent only 2 per cent of *all* households, these are the people who certainly feel the pain of a few interest rate increases.

I should add one further qualification: while it's clear that most people with negatively geared investment properties have plenty of equity in their own homes to fall back on, I won't be surprised if those who bought near the top of the market find themselves having lost money rather than made it if, as I fear, apartment prices in Sydney and Melbourne remain 'flat to down' for some years yet.

Putting it all together, I don't think we should bemoan the fact that people are continuing to borrow to buy their own homes. It's almost always a worthwhile move. Nor should we be too fearful about the large amount of debt they've acquired to do so. Remember that acquiring a large mortgage and spending the next 20 or 30 years paying it off is the way most Australians have saved most of what they have over their lifetimes (though the rise of compulsory superannuation will make this less true in future).

Saving, debt and guilt

Remember, too, that paying off your home as quickly as possible remains one of the best ways to invest any spare cash. That's because not many (safe) investments offer returns as high as the interest you pay on your mortgage. And the interest earnt on such investments is taxable, whereas interest paid on mortgages isn't tax deductible. So let's hope now the housing boom is behind us, more people will get back to paying off their home loans rather than adding to them.

As you've probably deduced, however, I'm not so relaxed about the greater use of borrowing via credit cards. So before we leave the subject of saving and debt, let me make sure you're abreast of some recent developments in this area—an understanding of which could help heavy credit-card users waste a bit less of their hard-earned on interest payments.

Until relatively recently, the banks' credit-card products proved strangely impervious to the increased competition unleashed by the deregulation of the banks in the mid-1980s. The banks charged remarkably high interest rates—which seemed to go up more than they came down—plus hidden 'merchant service fees' of up to 4 per cent to businesses accepting payment by credit card. Various banks also offered cards with no interest-free period and somewhat lower interest rates, but they weren't very popular. I suspect a lot of people con themselves, telling themselves it won't be long before they've paid off their arrears and will be able to take advantage of the interest-free period.

Throughout the 1990s the banks heavily promoted the use of credit cards, introducing frequent-flyer and other reward schemes to encourage us to put everything we bought on our cards. The amount we owed skyrocketed. But finally, in 2003, the Reserve Bank stepped in to try to inject more competition. It forced the banks to almost halve the fees they pay each other (and thus reduce the service fees paid by merchants), it stopped the credit-card companies—MasterCard and Visa—from prohibiting merchants from imposing a surcharge on customers who pay by credit card, and it obliged the card companies to admit non-bank institutions to their schemes.

Since these changes, credit cards have become less profitable to banks and they've been rethinking their approach. They still do well out of people who borrow and pay interest on their cards (known in the trade as 'revolvers'), but since the reduction in merchant service fees they now make little if anything out of people who pay their accounts in full each month (known as 'transactors'). Most banks cut back the generosity of their reward schemes and many increased their annual fees. Some encouraged their transactors to shift to American Express. And they may have become more inclined to keep their interest rates high.

But the banks are now exposed to new firms entering the credit-card market. The new entrants could seek to bid away the lucrative revolvers, while avoiding the unprofitable transactors (which the existing players were using their revolvers to cross-subsidise). The new players tend to offer low-interest rate, no-frills cards, with minimal fees and no reward schemes. Lenders such as Aussie Home Loans, Members Equity, BankWest and Wizard Home Loans are charging rates ranging between 10 and 13 per cent. These compare with standard cards charging between 16 and 18.5 per cent—a huge difference.

Saving, debt and guilt

But the existing banks haven't taken this lying down. Westpac, St George and ANZ, for instance, have introduced new cards charging around 11 per cent. (And it turns out that there are big banks behind several of the seemingly non-bank cards: Virgin is with Westpac, Aussie is with ANZ and Wizard is with the huge American finance company GE Consumer Finance.)

The trick for credit-card users is to be completely honest with themselves about whether they're revolvers (they pay interest) or transactors (they don't)—because the best strategy is different for the two groups. Transactors don't need to worry about the amount of the interest rate they're (not) being charged. Their focus should be on the length of the interest-free period, the size of their annual fee and the generosity of their reward scheme—taking care not to pay more for the reward scheme than it's worth to them. Roughly, it's worth the equivalent of 0.7 percentage points of interest rate.

As for revolvers, I can't think of any good reason why they shouldn't switch to one of the new low-interest cards. The amount of interest they're paying dwarfs the (modest) value of reward points and worries about the size of annual fees. The number of days of interest-free credit being offered isn't relevant because they never get *any* free credit. I'd be wary of choosing a low-rate card on the attractiveness of the 'honeymoon' deal (the short-term inducement to change cards) rather than on the level of the ongoing interest rate. Honeymoons end more quickly than you think. And people who flit from honeymoon to honeymoon get a bad credit rating.

Another trap—as Andrew Willink, of the financial services research firm Cannex, has pointed out—is the very low minimum payments some cards demand. An interest rate of 18 per cent a year is roughly equivalent to 1.5 per cent a month. So if you stuck to a minimum monthly payment of 1.5 per cent of the balance outstanding, you'd be repaying next to no principal and so would go on paying interest forever. A minimum payment of 2 per cent wouldn't be much better.

The unvarnished truth, of course, is that using credit cards to borrow is for mugs—young people who haven't learnt how to handle credit, and older victims of our consumption-obsessed society. The more pressing point, however, is that at least we're finally getting some competition into the credit-card market. But that competition will die unless enough revolvers overcome their inertia and move to the new, cheaper cards. So if you must use your card, at least be canny about it.

PART TWO

THE OUTSIDE WORLD

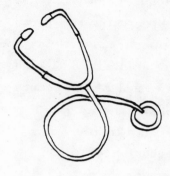

CHAPTER 7
Paying for health care

There's a paradox at the heart of Medicare. What we *hear* is unending complaints about its manifold and manifest inadequacies, the claim that it's in crisis. But what we *get* is health outcomes that compare favourably with other developed countries. So if the system really has been in crisis for all these years, it doesn't seem to be showing up in our health. I guess it's only natural for people to focus on the aspects of the system that aren't working well— and that's certainly the media's focus—but, before we launch into that, let's stand back for a broader perspective. We'll do so with the help of the most informative publications of the Australian Institute of Health and Welfare.

A second Medicare paradox is that, despite all the protests we hear about hospital cutbacks, we're spending more on health care, not less. A lot more. In 2003/04, the nation's total spending on health services reached $78 billion. That's about $3900 per person, and spending per person has grown by 3.4 per cent a year—in real terms—over the past 10 years. It's true that the number of beds available in acute-care hospitals has been cut since the 1980s, but this doesn't mean fewer people are being treated. Mainly because of the increase in day-surgery admissions, the average length of people's stay in acute-care hospitals has fallen from 4.6 days in 1993/94 to 3.4 days in 2003/04. So, despite the fewer beds, the number of patients has actually been growing at the rate of 3.8 per cent a year during the 2000s.

It's worth noting that 45 per cent of that $78 billion total spending was done by the Commonwealth and 23 per cent by state governments, leaving 32 per cent paid directly by you and me, either as health fund premiums or out-of-pocket payments. Our direct share is about as high as ever, despite the Howard Government's 30 per cent rebate on private insurance.

According to the institute's figuring, our spending of $3900 a year per person is on par with the $4000 per person spent by the Canadians and Germans, but still way below the $7600 spent by the Americans. On the other hand, our spending is well ahead of the $2500 per person spent by the New Zealanders, the $2100 spent by the British or the $2300 spent by the Japanese. So our spending is about average by the standard of developed countries.

The trick, however, is that the amount a country spends on health care isn't closely related to the quality of its citizens' health. The health of Americans, for instance, isn't twice as good as ours. It isn't even better. By the same token, our health isn't almost twice as good as that of the Brits. No, the factor

Paying for health care

that does most to explain the variance in countries' spending on health care is the system by which they pay their doctors and, in consequence, the incomes of their doctors. So, although our health isn't markedly better than the Brits', at least our doctors don't complain as much as theirs do.

When you think about it, you realise that almost all the public debate about health care involves arguments about the way we pay for it—the obsession with private insurance, for instance—or complaints from different parts of the system that the pollies aren't giving them enough money. And when you've got a gripe about your share of the pie, it's the easiest thing in the world to draw attention to yourself by alleging that 'the system is in crisis'.

But the truth is that over the course of the 1990s and early 2000s, our lives became measurably longer and healthier. We all know that the rate of infant mortality is one of the key measures of a nation's health and that infant mortality fell markedly in the early part of the last century, thereby doing much to increase longevity. But get this: over the 12 years to 2001, our infant mortality rate fell by a third, from 8 deaths per 1000 live births to 5.3. The main reason for that was the remarkable success of our campaign against sudden infant death syndrome. Since the program was introduced in 1991, the incidence of SIDS has dropped by two-thirds.

In 1970, Australia's life expectancy was 16th highest among the OECD countries. In 2001 it was third highest. The overall mortality rate fell by half between 1970 and 1999, which was faster than in every other high-income OECD country except Japan. Our decline in mortality rates in the five years to 2001 was the greatest five-year decline since 1923. Much of the improvement has been due to a fall in deaths from heart disease. This reflects both a fall in the incidence of heart attacks and better survival after heart attacks. In the period 1993/94 to 2000/01, the incidence of heart attacks for people aged 40 to 90 years fell by 23 per cent, and death from heart disease fell by a third.

Of course, the record of our improving health is not without blemishes. The most glaring is that death rates among Aborigines and Torres Strait Islanders have fallen only slightly in recent years and remain more than double those for non-Indigenous people. The other big worry is that we keep getting fatter. Between 1989 and 2001, overweight and obesity among those aged 18 and over rose from 32 per cent to 42 per cent for women and from 46 per cent to 58 per cent for men. More than half of Australians are insufficiently active to achieve a benefit to their health.

Overall, however, you'd have to say we're getting reasonable value for our health dollar. The complaints arise not because spending is falling, but because the politicians are preventing spending from growing as strongly as it would if they stopped trying to hold it back. Really? Why? Well, let's take a closer look at the health-care 'system'.

The very heart of the health-care problem is that we regard health as too important to be left to the market the way most other aspects of our lives are. We believe no one should be left to suffer illness or death simply because they can't afford health care. Marketplaces for any commodity are generally very efficient, but not very fair. We intervene in the health market to make it fairer, but we do so at the cost of efficiency. Though we're not prepared to leave health to the market, nor are we prepared to go to the opposite extreme of 'socialised medicine'. The result is a hybrid system of public provision (public hospitals) and public subsidies to private enterprise (doctors, private hospitals and pharmaceutical companies). The public hospitals have no incentive to be efficient, while the private-enterprise players have every incentive to over-service (which they get away with because their prices are so heavily subsidised). So our system has an inbuilt tendency to ever-increasing cost.

Another consequence of the hybrid system is that the way the community pays for its health care is tremendously complicated and diffuse. We pay through (small) direct out-of-pocket payments, the 1.5 per cent Medicare levy, private health insurance premiums and general federal and state taxation. This means there's little link between benefits and costs in most people's minds. Doctors think themselves heroes when they argue that their professional judgments about the treatments needed for their patients should be unfettered by cost considerations. Anyone who begs to differ is a money-obsessed beancounter. And the funding confusion means that much of the public debate about health care amounts to an endless game of pass-the-parcel. The vested interests are always lobbying the politicians to rejig the funding arrangements in their favour; the politicians are always seeking our votes by promising to rejig the funding arrangements in *our* favour.

The fundamental problem with health care is that we need to find a better trade-off between our conflicting objectives of equity and efficiency; to keep the system fair while making it less inefficient; to extract more value from the health dollar. But this would involve measures that harmed the interests of one or more of the powerful groups within the industry, so the politicians paper over the cracks by eternally fiddling with the funding arrangements, but generally keeping the lid on *government* spending on health care.

Why? Because, although they know most of us would like to see far more spent on health care than already is, they don't believe we're prepared to pay for it. Many in government also believe that, with the system in its current unsatisfactory state, any increase in public spending on health care they were prepared to allow would do a lot more to line the pockets of doctors and drug companies than to improve the nation's health.

Medicare has been highly popular with the public since its introduction by the Hawke Government in 1984. Technically, its great strength is on the equity side: universal coverage. Every Australian is entitled to the health care they need, regardless of their ability to afford it or their possession of insurance. In practice, however, it's likely that what appeals to most people is the illusion that it's free. Medicare guarantees 'free' access to public hospitals and, where it's available, bulk billing means 'free' access to doctors. Medicare's inception was accompanied by the introduction of the Medicare levy—a (then) 1 percentage point surcharge on taxable income. The modest proceeds of the levy, however, fall far short of covering the full cost of government spending on health care. Most of that comes from general federal and state tax revenue.

The introducers of Medicare made much of the fact that it made private health insurance unnecessary. What they didn't admit was that their calculations about Medicare's affordability

Paying for health care

rested heavily on the assumption that most people would continue their private insurance, making it a kind of voluntary tax. Over time, however, many people—particularly the healthy—gave up their insurance. As they did, the cost to the less-healthy people remaining rose rapidly, precipitating further rounds in the vicious circle of declining membership and rising premiums.

Partly because of this—and the increased patronage of public hospitals Medicare led to—but mainly because of the generally rapid rise in hospital costs, the Hawke Government soon reached the point where it could no longer afford to honour its promise of free public hospital admission to all comers. It didn't impose admission charges, however, but merely set a limit on the level of funds it was prepared to supply to public hospitals each year. With the state governments either unwilling or unable to take up the slack, the result was the advent of waiting lists—or, more meaningfully, waiting times—for elective surgery in public hospitals. While people often seek to explain the now ubiquitous waiting lists in terms of shortages of hospital beds, surgeons or operating theatres, it's important to understand that they represent nothing more than non-price rationing on the part of governments. One consequence, of course, is to drive those who can afford it back into the hands of the private health funds, in the process introducing a de facto two-class health system.

From the beginning, John Howard and the Liberals vigorously opposed Medicare, particularly bulk billing. Eventually, however, Mr Howard bowed to its great popularity and won election in 1996 with a core promise to preserve it. But this hasn't stopped him pursuing long-standing Liberal preoccupations. He used a range of sticks and carrots—including the hugely expensive 30 per cent tax rebate—to reverse the declining membership of private health funds and limit (to some extent) the continuing rise in their premiums.

Bulk-billing payments—or, alternatively, medical benefit rebates—are a set percentage of the 'schedule fee' nominated in the federal government's schedule of medical procedures. But the Howard Government's failure to raise schedule fees in line with the growing costs of running a medical practice led many GPs and specialists to set their own fees well above the schedule fee and to limit access to bulk billing, particularly in country areas. The resulting sharp decline in the proportion of bulk-billed consultations and sharp increase in out-of-pocket payments caused big public concern in the approach to the 2004 federal election. Mr Howard's eventual response—as modified by the Senate—was to patch up the incentives for doctors to bulk bill health-care card holders and children, while introducing a 'safety net' for families and others whose out-of-pocket payments exceeded certain levels in a particular year.

When you remember that Medicare itself was designed to be the safety net, this is a commentary on how far the ideal has slipped. The safety net proved to be far more costly to the government than originally expected, and so was set at a less-attainable level after the election. Initial experience also suggests that, contrary to what might have been expected, the safety net has benefited not the poor (who tend to avoid out-of-pocket payments by queuing in public hospitals) but the people who use the private system and live in better-class suburbs where doctors' out-of-pocket costs tend to be highest.

Paying for health care

Turning our minds to the future, the stark truth is that, where money is concerned, our health system is a bottomless pit. Our spending on health care is going to keep growing strongly, year after year, without end. And we're never going to reach a point where we feel we've spent enough. Why not? Partly because the population is ageing, but mainly because our desire for better health is insatiable.

Medical science will keep coming up with a steady stream of ways to prolong our lives and ensure the extra years are of high quality. Consider this list of wonderful advances, taken from the Productivity Commission's 2005 report on the Impacts of Medical Technology. Over the next 10 or 20 years, we can expect big advances in magnetic resonance and other imaging, the development of artificial organs and joints (including spinal discs, hearts, and pancreases for diabetics), image-guided brain surgery through small openings in the skull, other advances in minimally invasive procedures through computer-aided and robot-assisted surgery, the use of vaccines to prevent cancer, the development of artificial blood, genetic testing to identify susceptibility to cancer, heart disease and diabetes, gene therapy to replace, repair or alter our genes, computer-driven discovery and testing of new drugs, the emergence of 'biological' medicines (using proteins rather than chemicals) and personalised medicines, organ transplants from animals, and much more.

There's no doubt we'll want to leap onto every new 'breakthrough'. Trouble is, new medical technologies almost invariably involve a lot more expense. Sometimes new technology is more expensive because it's dearer than the technology it replaces. Other times, while the new approach lowers costs *per patient*, it's such an improvement and so much safer it's used on a lot more patients—including patients formerly judged to be too old. And then you've got new technology which, while it offers great benefits to patients in some circumstances, individual doctors choose to use in circumstances where the benefit is doubtful.

One way or another, we needn't be in any doubt that the cost of health care is going to keep rising strongly. And here's a further factor: it's a safe bet that, as our incomes grow in coming years, we'll be devoting a higher proportion of them to spending on health care. If we're richer we'll have to spend more on something, and health is a better thing than most other possibilities.

But most health care is financed by the public sector. So to say we're going to be spending an ever-growing amount on health care is to say we're going to be paying ever-rising taxes. Now, there's nothing terrible about that. Health care is a perfectly sensible thing to be spending more on and, particularly because of our desire to ensure it's made available on the basis of need rather than means, taxation is a perfectly sensible way to pay for it.

What is terrible is this: the bucket into which we're going to be pouring all this extra money leaks like mad. Our health system is quite inefficient and permits a lot of waste. Far too high a proportion of the extra money ends up fattening the incomes of health workers (particularly medical specialists) without doing much to give us better health. That's another respect in which health-care spending is a bottomless pit. Mixing metaphors, it's clear we ought to get a new bucket before we start pouring a lot more money into it.

Paying for health care

But what would such a more-value-for-money system look like? In Dr Vince FitzGerald's 2005 report to the Victorian Government, *Governments Working Together*, he tells us. He presents for debate an amalgam of the latest and best thinking by health economists and others about the completely new system we should work towards. It's one the Kiwis have already started adopting but, be warned, it's radical stuff.

The big problem with our health system is that it's so fragmented. This would be true even if responsibility weren't divided between the Commonwealth and the states. We look after different aspects of people's health out of different boxes: boxes for general practitioners, specialists, other health professions, public hospitals, private hospitals, the Medical Benefits Scheme, the Pharmaceutical Benefits Scheme, and aged care. This fragmentation means no one in the 'system' accepts ultimate responsibility for the total health needs of the individual. You can get doubling up, but you can also get people slipping between the cracks (such as when hospitals simply discharge sick people they don't believe they can help any further). So you get a lack of both coordination and continuity of care. You get huge scope for wasteful cost-shifting games and you don't necessarily get people receiving the most appropriate treatment from the most cost-effective source.

Dr FitzGerald argues that the answer to divided federal and state responsibilities is not for roles to be rationalised but for much greater cooperation between governments. To this end he suggests the setting up of a national Commonwealth and state body, the Australian Health Commission, to design, drive and monitor the reform process. The reform is introduction of a completely integrated health-care system. And the key element of the new system would be up to 30 'regional health agencies' across the country.

The federal and state governments would pool all the money they presently put into all those different boxes I mentioned and divide it up between the 30 regional health agencies. It would be divided on a per-head basis, after allowing for the known health characteristics of the people living in each region. Thus the regional agency would be the 'budget-holder'—it would hold all the money that any government was going to spend on health care or aged care for all the people in its region.

As the budget-holder—the 'purchaser'—it would purchase from 'providers' all the medical services needed by its people. Providers would include GPs, specialists, physiotherapists and all other allied health professionals, as well as public and private hospitals and private nursing homes. It would have contracts with GPs and other providers specifying how much it would pay for which services and the size of any co-payment they were permitted to charge on the top. Because it would hold all the public subsidy to be provided in a region, the agency would be in a strong position to bargain with providers.

The point of all this would be to improve accountability and incentives. The agencies would be accountable (possibly to their state government) if they overspent their budget or failed to maintain the health of their populations. They would have an incentive to avoid waste by always finding the most cost-effective way to deal with people's problems and to save money down the track by putting a lot more emphasis on prevention, health promotion and early diagnosis. They would shift the focus to the needs of particular patients rather than to outfits that care only about doing whatever it is they do.

This would be such a radical change it would have to be phased in over five or 10 years. You'd have to test it extensively through pilot programs before you rolled it out state by state. Not sure you like the sound of it or something like it? That's understandable. But the pressure for radical reform of the health system will come every time people look at their pay slips and see how much tax they're paying.

And while we're trembling on the brink, there's an element of that larger reform we could be getting on with independently. The realisation that prevention is better than cure—better for patients, better for taxpayers—is as old as Methuselah. So why, at this late stage of knowledge and know-how, are we doing so little prevention? There's a wealth of evidence that many health promotion and disease-prevention campaigns—public health programs—are highly cost-effective. That almost goes without saying for the anti-smoking campaign, since the ads, Quitline, the bans on tobacco advertising and the bans on smoking in buildings and on public transport were supplemented by hefty increases in the tax on cigarettes.

But the same is true of the rich countries' campaigns against HIV/AIDS, with the combination of advertising, education, promotion of condom use and, even more controversial, needle-exchange programs. Most immunisation programs are highly cost-effective, as are the various advances in the road safety campaign—including compulsory seatbelt-wearing and random breath-testing.

Not all preventative campaigns make sense, of course. Where the incidence of a particular disease is low, the cost of mass screening exceeds the benefits. And campaigns that involve a lot of advertising without offering concrete means of follow-up—such as that slob Norm and the Life Be In It campaign—don't yield lasting benefits.

You have to find the line between pressing people to take responsibility for their own bodies and actions and merely 'blaming the victim'. Where governments want to go through the motions without disturbing powerful commercial interests or imposing restrictions that may prove unpopular with sections of the public, that line hasn't been found. Note the many restrictions on our liberty governments have imposed—and we have happily accepted—in the past, such as bans on tobacco advertising and smoking in public places, prohibition of under-age drinking, compulsory seatbelt-wearing, speed limits, random breath-testing and many more. The politician who professes to be worried about childhood obesity, but won't contemplate banning the advertising of junk food on television, isn't dinkum.

But with all this evidence of success, why aren't we putting a lot more of our health resources into prevention rather than cure? Because the feds leave it to the states, and vice versa. Because the money we spend on curing illness is income for the providers of health care, who are highly vocal and well organised. Public health promotion involves the allied health professions—nurse educators, counsellors, dietitians, for instance—who are not powerful in the system.

Preventive medicine is an investment: you spend up front in the hope of benefits and savings down the track. In the annual struggle to keep the growth in total health spending within bounds, it's just too tempting to push public health promotion off into the never-never. The politics of health is such that, until the Treasury and Finance ministers impose preventive medicine on the medicos, they will go on wasting opportunities to give us better health for our health dollar. The fact that we're currently enjoying such favourable health outcomes despite the failings of our health-care system is no justification for continued waste and inefficiency.

CHAPTER 8

Taxes—love 'em or hate 'em

Moving on from health, and the importance of our tax dollars in supporting the health-care system, there are many other important and earnest things to be said about all the tax we pay. I want to talk first about what I reckon must be the greatest form of tax avoidance practised in this country. It's a technique engaged in much more by the poor than the rich. It's something that comes to people so naturally they don't know they're doing it. And, of course, it's completely and utterly legal. It's something the Poms call DIY—do-it-yourself.

The first qualification for exploiting this loophole is that you have to be handy around the house (which counts me out). But do-it-yourself is endemic. People on modest incomes (and the hard-pressed middle class) fix their own cars, do their own home maintenance, and all their own house painting. Young couples get a foothold in the property market by buying an old dump—which is all they can afford—and renovating it themselves. On a more mundane level, people mow their own lawns, cook their own meals rather than eat out, clean their own homes, and mind their own children.

Everyone knows that when you do it yourself you save money. That's why people do it themselves (though, of course, plenty of people *enjoy* doing certain things for themselves). But many people don't realise that one of the reasons they save money by doing things for themselves is that they're avoiding taxation. The loophole is that the government can tax only arm's-length transactions. When you pay someone to do something for you, that payment is taxed as income in the hands of the other person. So the price the other person charges is higher because he or she ends up with only part of what you've paid. If there were no such thing as income tax, the price you'd have to pay the other person would be lower. But when you do something yourself—when, in a sense, you pay yourself to do something for you—there's no arm's-length transaction and so no tax liability is incurred. And the tax you avoid is the main saving involved.

Really? Surely the main saving arises from the fact that your own labour comes free of cost—tax or no tax. No, not really. Just because you don't have to shell out money for something doesn't mean it's free of cost. As anyone who's had to be nagged to do household chores knows only too well, the cost of doing it yourself is the leisure time you have to give up to do it. This is an instance of what economists call 'opportunity cost'—the thing you've had to give up because you've chosen to do something else.

You can value your leisure at your after-tax hourly rate of income from your job. If you're the kind of person who does a lot of things for yourself, it's likely that the value of your leisure is quite a bit less than the hourly rate you'd have to pay a mechanic to fix your car, a painter to paint your house, or whatever. But why is the professional's hourly rate higher? Often, partly because the pro can do a better-quality job than you can. Almost certainly, because the pro can do the job faster than you can. But both those factors are built into your opportunity cost. You have to give up more hours of leisure than the pro would and you probably settle for a lesser-quality job. So what's the main saving from doing it yourself? The fact that your labour, unlike the professional's, is tax free.

When you look at it like this, you see why lower income-earners are more likely to engage in this form of tax avoidance than higher income-earners. Making the generous assumption that higher income-earners are just as handy as lower income-earners, the main difference between them is that higher income-earners are likely to set a higher value on their leisure time because their after-tax hourly income is higher. Doctors or lawyers or business executives are less likely to try DIY because their after-tax hourly income is usually higher than the hourly rate they'd have to pay a tradesperson to do it for them.

But there's another reason ordinary employees are more likely to do it themselves. They work for a fixed 38 hours a week plus the odd bit of overtime. Many would probably like to increase their income by working longer hours in their job. In the absence of that, they can achieve the same result—make their take-home pay stretch further—by doing jobs themselves rather than paying other people to do them. (A limitation of this analysis, by the way, is its assumption that all work, whether paid or at home, involves 'disutility'—that is, people don't enjoy doing it. In reality, many people enjoy work and some may regard work they do around the house as little different from leisure. But this just makes it more attractive to exploit the tax advantages of do-it-yourself.)

The most sublime example of tax avoidance through do-it-yourself is the person who gives up his job so he can build his own home. There's a lot of it about. Each year the New South Wales Government issues about 15 000 permits to owner-builders (though not all will have chucked in their jobs). When you give up your job, what you lose is not what the boss pays you but only your after-tax income. Then you're free to do it yourself rather than pay taxpaying sub-contractors to do it for you. Your labour goes completely untaxed. Whether it makes financial sense turns on whether what you lose by giving up your job is more or less than what you save by doing it yourself (remembering to allow for the likelihood that you'll take longer to do it and be rough around the edges). It's less likely to make sense for someone with a high-paying professional job; it's more likely to make sense for someone with a trade or blue-collar job. Once again, it's a form of tax avoidance more suited to lower income-earners than higher income-earners.

The greater scope for the lower-paid to avoid tax by doing it themselves is a leveller in our society. It isn't taken account of in conventional studies of the distribution of income between rich and poor. If it were, the gap wouldn't be as large as it seems. Thirty years ago, my observation that some people save money by choosing to cook their own meals, clean their own homes and mind their own children would have struck you as odd. It's not so odd now that so many married women have returned to the (paid) workforce.

Two-income couples have, to a greater or lesser extent, made the opposite choice, of paying other people to mind their kids and clean their houses, and paying the local take-away to cook their meals. Why? Because, leaving aside the self-fulfilment that women derive from employment outside the home, they have figured that the after-tax income they earn from paid employment exceeds the cost of paying others to do things they formerly did for themselves. Except in the case of child-minding, the couple could, of course, struggle on doing everything themselves. But often they don't. Why not? Because as they give up more time to doing paid work, the value they place on their diminished leisure time rises. The opportunity cost of continuing to do everything yourself becomes too high.

But if taxation plays such a large, if unacknowledged, part in people's decisions about do-it-yourself, how does that square with the cash economy? Many of the people we could pay to mow lawns, clean houses or mind kids don't bother paying tax. Here we're dealing with a combination of tax avoidance (which is legal) on the householder's part and tax evasion (which isn't) on the part of the service-providers. If the people we could pay to do work for us aren't paying tax on their income, that diminishes the amount of tax we could avoid by choosing to do the work ourselves, but it doesn't eliminate it.

The people who come to our doors offering to do work for cash neither pocket all the illicit saving nor pass all of it on to us. Competition between such people prevents them from keeping all of the saving and obliges them to pass some of it on to their customers. So, although you avoid most tax when you choose to do it yourself rather than pay someone whose prices reflect the fact that he or she is paying the full whack of tax, you still avoid some tax when you choose to do it yourself rather than pay someone whose prices reflect the fact that he or she is on the fiddle.

Of course, no amount of tax avoidance through DIY could change the fact that we're still paying a mighty lot of it—more than we used to. The burden of taxation has been growing inexorably for many decades. In each of the 1980s and 1990s, the level of total federal and state taxes (not just income tax) rose by 2 percentage points (about $20 billion in today's dollars) of gross domestic product (GDP) per decade. That has occurred as politicians have responded to the public's insatiable demand for more government services—more health care, more education, more defence and security, more law and order, more lots of other things. Following the Whitlam Government's famous blowout, it's actually kept on going under the succeeding Labor and Liberal governments. And that's despite the burgeoning user charges.

But if the Howard Government's so widely criticised for starving worthy causes, despite pulling in a record level of taxes, where on earth is the money going? The short answer is: almost everywhere. There are no one or two areas that have benefited hugely while everywhere else has been starved. Spending on defence and security is up, obviously, but this accounts for little of the increase. Spending on roads is up—though no one from the country would have noticed. The most you can say is that John Howard has spent the past 10 years scattering presents on a fair number of 'special friends': single-income couples with young children, people who send their kids to private schools, people with private health insurance, the alleged self-funded retirees and people who derive income from capital gains. One conclusion you can draw is that Howard is so fond of handing out special tax breaks to favoured groups that he can rarely afford much in the way of a general income-tax cut.

However, to acknowledge that we're paying more tax than ever is not to say we're *highly* taxed. To get to the truth about how much we're taxed, remember that income tax accounts for only a bit more than a third of all the tax we pay. So if we want the full story we need to look at the combined burden of all the taxes we pay, federal and state. According to OECD figures, our total taxation in 2003 was equivalent to 31.6 per cent of GDP. That makes us the eighth lowest-taxing country among the 30 members of the OECD (and the other seven include two developing countries we don't usually compare ourselves with: Mexico and South Korea). Our total burden of 31.6 per cent of GDP compares with Canada 33.8 per cent, New Zealand 34.9, Britain 35.6, Germany 35.5, France 43.4, Denmark 48.3, and Sweden 50.6 per cent. The only major countries lower than us are the United States on 25.6 per cent and Japan on 25.3 per cent. But both countries have been through recessions that we haven't and both have huge budget deficits their taxpayers aren't being asked to cover.

You only need to look in the annual budget papers to see what governments do with all the taxation they collect and to see that most of it goes on the things we think it should. Even so, I suspect many of us feel we pay a lot without getting much back. In truth, however, most people get a lot more back than they imagine and many get back more than they give. Most of us are aware that one of the main roles of the budget is to redistribute income from the better-off to the less well-off. But most wouldn't realise how much redistribution occurs. And we're even less well informed about the way the budget effectively shifts our income over our life cycle, taking more than it gives at some points in our life but doing the reverse at other points.

Consider the results of a study by Professor Ann Harding and Rachel Lloyd, of the University of Canberra's Natsem Centre, and Professor Neil Warren of the University of New South Wales. It was based on estimates for 2001/02 and divided households into the eight 'ages of man' (and woman): young singles (up to 35 years), young couples (under 35) with no kids, couples with the eldest kid under 5 years, couples with their eldest between 5 and 14, couples with their eldest between 15 and 24, 'empty-nesters' (couples aged 55 to 64, with no dependent kids), older couples of age pension age, and aged singles (mainly widows).

The study started with these life cycle groups' 'private income' (from wages and investments) and added the cash benefits they received (from Austudy, the dole, various types of pension and family benefits) to get their 'gross income'. From gross income it subtracted each group's income tax and the federal indirect taxes they paid (the GST and excises on petrol, alcohol and tobacco), then it added estimates of the value of government benefits in kind (education, health care, housing, child-care subsidies, aged care and others) to give an estimate of each group's 'final income'. Note that the study was unable to take account of all taxes (it missed federal corporate taxes and state taxes) and all government spending (missing spending on defence, law and order, transport and communications). But it captured roughly equal proportions of taxation and spending.

Starting with private income, we find that, on average, young singles pulled in about $630 a week. Once they've become couples their combined private income averaged $1390 a week. But once the first kids come along, with dad getting promoted but mum less likely to be working full-time, their average combined income fell to less than $1100 a week. As the kids start going to school and mum does more paid work, however, the couples' income recovered to $1160 a week, reaching a peak of $1400 a week when the eldest kid is 15 or more. For empty-nesters, average combined income fell to $680 a week because of voluntary and involuntary early retirement. Once couples were of pension age their *private* income fell to an average of $290 a week and once one partner died it fell to just $150.

But now we need to see how these privately earnt sums were topped up by government pensions and cash benefits. Young singles got Austudy or dole payments averaging just $30 a week, while young childless couples got next to nothing. But couples with dependent children got family benefits averaging between $110

Taxes—love 'em or hate 'em

and $130 a week. Empty-nesters got dole or disability pensions worth an average of $110, while couples of pension age averaged $270 a week and aged singles $180.

Turning to tax payments, working singles and couples lost an average of about 22 per cent of their gross income in income tax, but this fell to 6 or 7 per cent for the retired. Working singles and couples lost about 9 per cent of their gross incomes through GST and excise, but for the retired the proportion rose to 10 or 12 per cent.

Now the really surprising one: benefits in kind. The cost to government of schools (public and private) was equivalent to a benefit to families with school-age children worth an average of $220 a week. The cost to government of higher education translated to a benefit to students worth up to $80 a week. The total cost to government of health care (including hospitals, Medicare rebates, pharmaceutical benefits and the private insurance rebate) worked out to be worth roughly $30 a week per adult or child, but leapt to more than $50 per person for empty-nesters and $100 to $120 per person for the aged.

Putting it all together, we find that, on average, young singles paid about $110 a week more in taxes than they got back in benefits, while young childless couples paid $320 a week more than they got back. Among couples with children, those with young kids lost a net $80 a week whereas those with older kids got back $90 to $110 a week more than they paid. The empty-nesters roughly broke even, while aged couples got back $450 a week more than they paid and aged singles got back a net $300.

See how it works? When you're single or part of a young couple, the system requires you to subsidise everyone else. When you've got a few school kids you get back a bit more than you put in, but when you're old and sick you really clean up.

How is it we rarely if ever hear politicians alluding to those kinds of results? Because most of us like to fantasise about paying less tax while getting more government services, and modern politicians' idea of leadership is to pander to our delusions. Particularly during election years, they pretend to be able to do the impossible. Little wonder we experience so many broken promises, so much disillusion and cynicism. The truth, as we've seen, is that notwithstanding all the efforts to restrict outlays, government spending keeps growing at a rate that's faster than the real growth in the economy. And notwithstanding all the alleged 'tax cuts' we're given, taxation collections keep growing in line with the growth in public spending.

How do the pollies manage this illusion? As we'll see in a moment, mainly by the presence of bracket creep and the absence of annual indexation of the tax scales. All the 'cuts' we keep hearing about—whether in government spending or in taxes—never bring us closer to the holy grail of Smaller Government, they merely slow the expansion of big government.

But here's where I cast off the politicians' mantle of hypocrisy. Their dishonesty about what's actually happening to public finances is a bad thing, but the rise in the tax 'burden' is good, not bad. Why? Because it's paying for things that are worth having— things that are better delivered by governments than by private enterprise.

What's more, there seems little doubt we'll be paying more tax, not less, as the years progress. And that, too, will be a good thing. In 2004, a former senior econocrat under Liberal and Labor governments, Dr Mike Keating, wrote a paper with a shocking title: 'The case for increased taxation'. He started by reminding us of the Howard Government's Intergenerational Report on the ageing of the population. It estimated that, on present policies, *federal* government spending is likely to rise by about 5 percentage points of GDP over the next 40 years. That's equivalent to about $50 billion a year in today's dollars—and it's over and above the rise necessary to keep federal spending growing as fast as the rest of the economy. A similar exercise by the Victorian Government estimated that *state* governments' spending is likely to rise by 4 percentage points of GDP over the same period. That's $40 billion a year on top of all the growth needed to preserve the states' present share of the economy.

When you get down to cases, you see that population ageing is just one of the factors that will require increased government spending—and not necessarily the biggest. In fact (and as discussed in the previous chapter), most of the extra spending foreseen by the Intergenerational Report came not from ageing but from increased health care for all of us.

We live in an age of continuous improvement in medical technology. As each year passes, doctors can do more to prolong our lives and, more to the point, prolong our active, healthy lives. Only trouble is, it makes health care ever more expensive. But think about it. As individuals get richer over time, they tend to devote more of their income to health care. It's the same for societies—the richer the country, the more money it devotes to health care. Is this a bad thing? Of course not. It merely reflects our priorities. We prefer living to dying.

It's a similar story with another major area of public spending, on education and training. Though we'll have fewer young people to educate, it's a safe bet that, overall, we'll be spending more rather than less in this area. A higher proportion of kids will go on to higher education, a higher proportion of uni graduates will do further degrees, and faster change in the structure of the economy will require more retraining. Is this bad? No—more education and training leads to more skilled jobs. And skilled jobs are not only better paid, they're cleaner, safer and more interesting.

Along with much greater outlays on health and education we can expect increased spending on repairing the environment (salinity, rivers, greenhouse gases and more), on updating public infrastructure (which we've tended to let run down in recent decades) and possibly on defence and security. It's possible that some of this increased spending could be met by increased user charging (full uni fees, private health insurance etc.) rather than higher taxes, but it's impossible to imagine that all or even most of it could be met that way.

But even if user charges and private provision *could* be used to avoid any great rise in the tax burden, it would involve changing Australia into a very different society to the one we've known. One where the less privileged were given much less support from the rest of the community. One that was much closer to requiring everyone to fend for themselves. Although the politicians' election antics discourage us from thinking clearly about these things, I doubt if that's what most of us want.

When you remember how reluctant politicians are to introduce new taxes—even the dreaded GST was largely a replacement for various other indirect taxes—how on earth will they be able to raise all the extra tax revenue they'll need? That's easy: bracket creep. (Let me whisper this so it doesn't frighten the horses.) Bracket creep is almost universally condemned by commentators and opposition politicians, but I think it's unjustly maligned.

Most of what the critics say about bracket creep is true, of course. It's true that the effect of inflation and real wage rises on the progressive income-tax scale causes the rate of tax we pay to rise over time. It's true the 'tax cuts' the politicians are always awarding just before elections only give us back our own money, money they've come by thanks to bracket creep. It's equally true that, whatever the pollies say, they never give back *all* the extra tax they gain from bracket creep, just some of it. And even if they did return it all on some particular occasion, it would still be true that the bracket-creep process started again on the day of the tax cut and would have completely eroded the value of the cut within a few years.

About the only dishonest thing I've heard said about bracket creep came from Treasurer Peter Costello. He was running the line that everyone earning between $21 600 and (now) $70 000 a year hadn't suffered from bracket creep because they hadn't been pushed up out of the 30 per cent tax bracket. That's a politician's favourite kind of statement: literally true, but highly misleading. Contrary to what the term 'bracket creep' implies, you don't have to be pushed into a higher bracket to suffer a rise in your overall rate of tax. All that's necessary to raise your *average* rate of tax is for a higher proportion of your income to be taxed at your existing 'marginal' rate of tax, which is always higher than the rates at which the earlier slices of your income were taxed.

The theoretical point to remember is this: the only way to completely eliminate bracket creep is for the government to index all the tax brackets automatically, in full, every year. Anything less than that involves the politicians deciding they're going to keep some of the proceeds of bracket creep and give some back, with the split-up to be entirely at their discretion.

Now, this is the point where I'm supposed to convince you that it's all very very evil, and demand the government institute full tax indexation forthwith. You're supposed to be convinced that bracket creep operates solely for the benefit of grasping politicians and completely contrary to the interests of taxpayers like you and me.

But that's a load of tosh. At its best, it displays a quite nerdish view of human nature and of the unwritten contract between governments and the governed.

If you look at what we do rather than what we say—at our 'revealed preference', as economists call it—you quickly realise we prefer to be taxed in less visible ways. Paying more tax isn't so bad if you don't notice it. And the beauty of bracket creep is that it sneaks up our taxes almost unnoticed. What could be less painful? One of the troubles with the economic rationalists is that they're too rational. They assume the rest of us are rational (which we aren't) and that making the world work in a more rational way would make us happier (which it wouldn't).

They can't get it through their logical skulls that most of us prefer a bit of illusion. Bracket creep is one example, but another is bulk billing. Why are so many of us so attached to bulk billing? Because we quite like the illusion that it makes going to the doctor free.

Of course, no one likes paying more tax just for the sake of it. And the denigrators of bracket creep play on this, acting as though the politicians simply trouser the money they rip off us by their nefarious ways. The critics want us to see ourselves solely as reluctant taxpayers, forgetting we're also citizens who—as we've seen—use the many and varied services governments provide to us and our children. They want us to unthinkingly assume we could all pay less tax without this involving any decline in the quality of health care and public education.

But the truth is that, opinion polling reveals that a growing majority of us are making the link between how much tax we pay and the quality of the hospitals and schools we rely on. According to careful and repeated polling by academics at the Australian National University, since the mid-1990s the proportion of people preferring reduced taxes has fallen by 30 percentage points, whereas the proportion preferring increased social spending has risen by 30 points.

I think it's fair to assume, however, that most people would find passing up a tax cut easier to accept than an explicit tax increase. That's the point about bracket creep: it's the least painful way for the politicians to deliver us better schools and hospitals. If we did have full tax indexation, and explicit tax increases were needed to pay for expanded and improved public services, it's likely those increases would be infrequent and our public hospitals and schools would be in even worse shape than they are.

The more ideological of the campaigners against bracket creep understand this, but are confident they'd be better off in such a world. They'd pay less tax, there'd be less requirement on them to subsidise people less well-off than themselves, and they're confident of their ability to afford private health and education and avoid the public squalor. If you don't like the sound of that world—or don't think you'd be among the winners—remember that bracket creep is just a harmless self-deception helping to keep it at bay.

CHAPTER 9
Crime and drugs

We're all terribly worried about crime, but I'm yet to be convinced our concern is genuine (or justified). It's my job in the media that makes me sceptical. It's just so obvious that there's a quid to be made from crime. As the commercial imperative drives the media ever further in the direction of news as entertainment, they devote more space and time to reporting and earnestly debating crime. So it's hard to avoid the suspicion that the media's customers actually enjoy feeling fearful about the (usually exaggerated) risk of being a victim of crime. Otherwise, why wouldn't they shun such unsettling news? Why do so many people lap up news about crime the way teenagers enjoy a really scary horror movie?

It's clear that, despite their repeated professions of concern, our politicians aren't sincere in their desire to reduce the rate of crime. They see it not as a crime problem, but as a political problem. They don't want to reduce crime as much as be seen to be *trying* to reduce it. So the solutions they apply aren't the ones recommended by the experts as likely to work, but the ones urged on them by the public and the media. And the solutions we urge on them are those that offer instant relief to our fears—or feed our desire for retribution. If we were more sincere in our desire to see less crime we'd be willing to pay the price: to spend more time thinking about what works and what doesn't, and to accept solutions which, although they provide less instant gratification of our emotions, are more likely to reduce the problem.

If you're prepared to engage your intellect, a good place to start is a paper on strategic approaches to property crime control by Dr Don Weatherburn, director of the New South Wales Bureau of Crime Statistics and Research, and Professor Peter Grabosky, of the Australian National University. Every year in Australia about one in 20 households are broken into, about one in 50 people have their car stolen and about one in 100 have something taken from them by violence or the threat of violence. Pat Mayhew of the Australian Institute of Criminology has estimated that the two most common forms of property crime—household burglary and car theft—cost the community more than $2.5 billion a year.

So property crime is something we should try to control. But how? Just about the first solution we think of is to increase the penalties for crime. Does it work? There's little research evidence that longer jail terms have much effect. Take the 'natural experiment' conducted in New South Wales with the introduction of 'truth in sentencing' under the *Sentencing Act* of 1989. This caused prison terms to increase across the board by between 25 and 33 per cent. The prison population rose from 4000 to 6500 in three or four years. But the five years following the introduction of the Act produced little sign that it had made much difference to crime rates.

Studies of the deterrent effect of increased penalties generally show them to be quite small. One recent study of rates of recidivism among drink-drivers following a doubling of the maximum penalty found no effect on drink-drivers in Sydney and only a slight reduction among those in the country. Laboratory experiments suggest tougher penalties aren't likely to function as a deterrent unless potential offenders think there is some reasonable prospect of apprehension. But for every 110 reports of break and enter in New South Wales during 2004, only one person went to prison.

This leads on to another of our favourite solutions: increase the number of police on patrol. Does it work? A US study found that a 10 per cent increase in police numbers produces a 3 per cent drop in serious crime. Making the brave assumption that this result would hold for Australia, a 20 per cent reduction in crime would require the hiring and training of more than 10 000 additional police officers in New South Wales alone—an increase in police numbers of two-thirds—which would increase the cost of the police force by $860 million a year. So this solution would be highly expensive—and raises the question of whether a different response to crime would be more cost-effective.

If the obvious, direct ways of trying to reduce property crime are weak on cost-effectiveness, it's time we tried something less obvious and less direct. In the jargon of the management consultants, it's time we tried a more 'strategic' approach. One important research finding is that, although a small number of individuals account for a disproportionate share of property crime, a surprisingly high number of people—mainly young people—engage in it occasionally. The fundamental solution to the willingness of so many young people to engage in crime involves major economic and social change—reducing poverty, parental neglect, family conflict and poor school performance.

Even if we could achieve all that, it would take a long time to work. What we could do much more quickly and easily, however, is reduce the frequency with which individuals offend by increasing the risks and reducing the opportunities. For instance, we could do more to make it harder to convert stolen property into cash. In some states there is no formal requirement for people to provide proof of identity or proof of ownership when they pawn goods or sell them to second-hand dealers. And even where those requirements do exist, the police could do a lot more checking and follow-up of pawnbrokers' records. Similarly, we could do a lot to discourage car theft if governments required the labelling of component parts and if it were harder to transfer vehicle compliance plates from wrecks bought at auctions (used to give stolen cars a new identity).

On a different tack, we should remember the value of methadone treatment for heroin users. A number of studies provide clear evidence that methadone maintenance treatment reduces the frequency of involvement in property crime. Once we start thinking more widely, the possibilities for reducing criminal opportunity and incentive are considerable. According to research findings, boredom among juveniles provides a major incentive for car theft; poor vehicle security provides a major source of opportunity for the same offence; youth homelessness appears to increase the frequency of shoplifting; agreed-value insurance policies provide opportunities for car insurance fraud; and poor choice of location and poor design of retail stores can provide abundant opportunities for retail-sector crime.

Australia's most prevalent crime is burglary, with 4 or 5 per cent of households being burgled each year—a rate that's high by international standards. But only about 6 per cent of reported burglaries are cleared up. We're dealing with a veritable industry here. So if we're interested in doing more to reduce burglary, and willing to use our brains, it would be useful to study the economics of that industry. Dr Richard Stevenson of Macquarie University, and colleagues from the New South Wales Bureau of Crime Statistics and Research, did this. They interviewed 267 imprisoned burglars in New South Wales jails and juvenile detention centres. (This means, by the way, that the study's results are biased towards the activities of professional burglars, ignoring the infrequent amateurs.)

So what have we discovered about the life and work of the industry's operatives? Well, it's a young man's game. Almost half the respondents were juveniles—which was necessary because juveniles constitute a significant majority of all burglars (this includes many thousands of kids who offend only once or twice in their lives, and are never caught). On average, the respondents had been nine months in detention and the majority had been free for at least six months before that. Even so, almost two-thirds said they didn't give any thought to the likelihood of getting caught. Most had been charged with four burglaries in their lives, though nearly a quarter had been charged with more than 20. Against this, the respondents typically admitted to actually committing eight or nine burglaries a month.

The study confirms what many of us have suspected: most frequent offenders are motivated by the need to generate money to pay for drugs. More than 90 per cent said they were users of illicit drugs. In general, the adults were hooked on heroin and the juveniles on marijuana. The rate at which individuals committed burglaries was closely related to their rate of spending on drugs. Most required a median of $1000 a week to support their habit (though heroin users spent a median of $1500 a week). They could never have supported this from their legal incomes, which averaged only $140 a week, mainly social security payments. Their incomes from the proceeds of burglary ranged from $600 to $4000 a week, with a median of $2000.

The study gave most attention to identifying the avenues through which burglars dispose of their loot. The surprise was how many means they used—four, on average—and that the most common was trading the stolen goods directly for drugs. What do the drug dealers do with the stuff? Many of the respondents were reluctant to say or didn't know (and didn't want to). But it seems the dealers keep it, sell it or give it to family and friends, and sometimes trade it with higher dealers.

The next most common means of disposal was sale or gift to family, friends and acquaintances. Then came sale to a professional fence. But the fourth method was a surprise: sale to a legitimate business. Seventeen per cent of respondents said they sold to a business most of the time and another 21 per cent said they did it some of the time. In nearly all cases, the respondent claimed the business knew the goods were stolen. The most frequently used businesses were corner stores, which bought cigarettes and similar goods for sale through the business, and other things (such as jewellery, electrical goods and clothing) for sale through an extensive network of family, friends and acquaintances. Jewellery stores were used frequently; they reset the stones and melted down the gold. The final common method of disposal was sale to pawnbrokers and second-hand dealers. But many regarded this as a last resort, partly because prices were lower and also because of the higher risk of police detection. The study found it *wasn't* common for burglars to hawk their stuff direct to strangers in pubs and clubs or on the streets.

What did they do to avoid being caught with stolen property? They dealt only with people they knew and trusted. They'd phone before making contact, avoid being seen or acting nervously, conceal the goods in a rucksack, avoid leaving fingerprints, use a scanner to overhear police radio messages and carry fake identification. But they also disposed of the goods remarkably rapidly—often within an hour. Even so, many said they were more concerned about being caught buying drugs than being caught with stolen property.

Another surprise was how often the respondents claimed to be stealing goods to order. Almost a third said they did this most of the time and almost another half did it some of the time. Orders varied from the general ('any consumer electricals') to the highly specific, where an item in a certain property would be specified. One respondent claimed that a jeweller gave him details of clients who'd purchased expensive jewellery, so he could steal it back. But most orders came from friends or family, followed by drug dealers and fences. Using the examples of a ring, a VCR and a power tool, the study established that the prices burglars obtained for stolen goods were usually only a quarter to a third of their price as new—thus leaving a fat profit margin for the receivers.

Dr Stevenson and his colleagues concluded that the market for stolen goods was 'efficient, adaptable, profitable and relatively low risk'. It was efficient and adaptable because burglars had a wide range of ways to dispose of goods. They could do so quickly, partly because they traded for drugs and partly because the thefts had been commissioned. The prices they obtained for stolen goods were low, but this still left room for both them and their receivers to make substantial profits. The incentive to be a receiver was high. In contrast, the risks for those stealing or buying stolen goods seemed small. If the clear-up rate for burglary was only 6 per cent, it was obvious that most thefts went undetected. The clear-up rate for receiving stolen goods wasn't known, but would be 9 per cent at most.

So what ideas for reducing the burglary problem does the study bring to mind? The authors came up with four. First, confirmation of the close link between burglary and drugs (including the drug dealers so often acting as receivers) suggested a need for a lot more cooperation between the police who specialise in drug detection and those responsible for general law enforcement. Second, the adaptability of burglars in using different methods of disposal suggested that police need to conduct surveillance on a wider range of outlets and be equally adaptable. Third, tougher penalties for receiving stolen goods—where at present only 6 per cent of those convicted are sent to prison—might help a bit by increasing the risks and strengthening social norms against accepting stolen property. Finally, the study underlined the findings of other studies that spending on drug treatment—methadone, etc.—was an effective way of reducing property crime as well as heroin consumption.

In response to evidence that heroin users commit less crime when on methadone than when they're off it, the New South Wales Government expanded its methadone program in 2000. It also tightened the law on selling goods to second-hand dealers or pawnbrokers, so that now you do need proof of identity and ownership. More significantly, it followed the Western Australian Government lead of letting police inspect pawnbroker transaction slips on line, rather than manually. This makes the enforcement process a lot more efficient.

One consequence of the immense media attention given to crime is to leave the public with an exaggerated impression of its prevalence and the probability of the individual being affected by it. For example, when psychologists ask people whether they think murder or suicide is the more common, most people are confident it's murder. In truth, suicide outnumbers murder by far. Most people believe murder to be more common because murders get far more publicity in the media. To be blunt, they're more interesting. Many suicides go unreported by the media because the person involved isn't well known, to respect the family's wish for privacy, or to avoid encouraging copy-cats.

Many people don't realise that the media don't see it as any part of their job to give their customers—that is, their readers, listeners or viewers—an accurate or balanced picture of what's happening in the world. Rather, the media trawl through all the ordinary, unremarkable, even boring things that happen to most of us most of the time, searching for the unrepresentative: the unusual, the extreme, the violent, the disputatious, the upsetting. These are the events the media consider to be 'newsworthy'—interesting—and so these are what they serve up to us.

For a less sensational but more accurate view of crime, I recommend Dr Weatherburn's excellent primer, *Law and Order in Australia: Rhetoric and Reality*. Weatherburn confirms that most of us think crime is rising and that this perception isn't much influenced by the statistical facts of the matter. We feel a lot more insecure than we did 20 years ago and, according to a survey of 17 developed countries in 2000, we have the second-highest proportion of people saying they feel 'very unsafe' walking alone at night in their local area.

The national figures for reported crime are incomplete, but they show that the rates of the most common crimes—household break and enter and car theft—more than doubled between the mid-1970s and the end of the 1980s. Turning to less common but more serious crimes, the rate of robbery (stealing something from someone with violence or the threat of it) more than doubled, while the rate of serious assault almost quadrupled over the same period.

With homicide, the national rate rose a little during the 1960s and 1970s, but has been fairly steady since then at two per

Crime and drugs

100 000 of population per year, and appeared to fall a fraction during the 1990s. Australia's biggest drug problem over the past 20 years or more has been heroin. The rate of heroin overdose increased about tenfold during the 1980s and 1990s. The use of cocaine and amphetamines rose in the five years to 1998. Since the early 1980s, the proportion of fatally injured drivers who had a blood alcohol content in excess of the legal limit has fallen from more than 40 per cent to less than 30 per cent.

OK, so what's the risk of becoming a victim of these crimes? For very common crimes the risk is, obviously, higher: about one in 20 households are broken into each year, while about one in 60 households each year experience a car theft. But it's not the same risk for everyone. For instance, the rate of break and enter in Bourke is almost seven times higher than for the rest of New South Wales. And those who suffer one break-in in a year are at a much higher risk of suffering several. With car theft, you're six times more likely to lose your motor vehicle in inner Sydney than you are in northern New South Wales. You're five times less likely to have your car stolen if it has an engine immobiliser. And you're six times more likely to have your car stolen if it's a Subaru Impreza WRX rather than a Holden Barina SB.

From official surveys that ask people if they've been victims of crime in the past 12 months, the victim of assault knows the offender in 60 per cent of cases. In the national survey of violence against women, only about 11 per cent of cases of sexual assault involved strangers. Despite the increase in the number of robberies, only one person in 170 falls victim each year. But the risk is about twice as high in New South Wales (one in 100) as in other states. It's much higher among teenagers (one in 50) than among people 35 and older (one in 250).

Putting it all together, although the level of crime is significantly higher today than it was in the 1960s, it tended to reach a plateau during the 1990s. Although the most common forms of property crime are more prevalent in Australia than in many developed countries, the problem's nowhere near as bad as talkback radio would have us believe. And here's the good news: the Crime Wave is receding. There's now no doubt about it. The tide turned in 2001 and there's been a general decline in *property* crime each year since then. The fall is occurring in every state, but seems concentrated in the bigger cities.

In New South Wales, the figures for recorded crime over the 24 months to December 2004 showed that crime fell in nine of the sixteen major categories. In the remaining seven categories— including murder and the various forms of assault—the level of crime was stable. So it's predominantly a fall in crime against property. In round figures, theft of motor vehicles fell by 5 per cent. The crimes of stealing from motor vehicles, stealing from homes, breaking and entering homes, and robbery with a weapon other than a firearm were each down by about 10 per cent. The crimes of stealing from the person (including pick-pocketing and bag-snatching without violence), shoplifting, breaking and entering some building other than a home, and robbery without a weapon (mugging) were each down by about 20 per cent. Looking at the four years to the end of 2004, the overall level of property crime in New South Wales fell by 36 per cent and is now below what it was in 1990.

Crime and drugs

Well, that's great news. But the obvious question is, why? Together with two researchers at the New South Wales Bureau of Crime Statistics, Steve Moffatt and Neil Donnelly, Dr Weatherburn has conducted a study of the causes of the decline. It began after the onset of a significant fall in the availability of heroin in early 2001, and it seems this is a major part of the explanation. At that time, the price of heroin in Sydney rose by 75 per cent to $380 a gram and the purity of heroin on the street fell from 70 per cent to about 30 per cent. Effectively, the price of heroin roughly quadrupled.

There followed an immediate drop in the number of fatal heroin overdoses which, along with other evidence, suggests a decline in the consumption of the drug prompted by the huge rise in its price. Because the decline in crime began at about the same time as the heroin drought and the fall in consumption, and because heroin users often resort to property crime—particularly robbery—to finance their purchases, it's reasonable to conclude that the fall in heroin consumption does a lot to explain the decline in crime. Some further circumstantial evidence: the drop in property crime has been concentrated in urban areas where heroin dependence is most prevalent.

But there has to be more to it, particularly because property-crime rates continued falling long after heroin consumption had stabilised at a lower level. One wrinkle is that there was actually a brief jump in the number of robberies immediately after the onset of the heroin shortage. And this spike coincided with a sharp rise in the percentage of suspected overdose fatalities in Sydney involving people who tested positive for cocaine.

Cocaine tends to be injected more frequently than heroin, making the habit much more expensive to maintain. Also, prolonged and frequent use of cocaine tends to make users more violent. But before long cocaine, too, became more costly and harder to get. Finally, about a year after the heroin shortage began, the number of re-registrations for methadone treatment increased significantly. And research confirms that addicts offend at a lower rate when they're in methadone maintenance treatment. Putting it all together, it seems that when the shortage of heroin made it more expensive, some users briefly turned to cocaine and undertook more robberies to cover its higher cost. When the price of cocaine rose also, some may have moved back on to methadone, causing a further decline in property crime.

But what about the role of policing and the courts—do they get any of the credit? A little. The study revealed no increase in the number of suspected offenders charged with robbery or burglary. But it did find an increase in the proportion of convicted burglars given a jail sentence. It also found that average jail sentences lengthened for both burglary and robbery.

Statistical tests couldn't detect any benefit from the longer sentences for robbery, but they did find that greater use of imprisonment for burglary offenders contributed to the decline in crime. Note, however, that this may have been less a deterrent effect than an 'incapacitation effect'. That is, offenders were able to burgle fewer homes because they spent more time behind bars. Of course, it costs the taxpayer a bundle to keep offenders locked up, so a separate question is whether dishing out more and longer sentences is a cost-effective way of controlling crime.

Crime and drugs

Finally, the strong growth in the economy seemed to help reduce crime. After controlling for all the other factors, tests showed a contribution from the growth in real incomes and the fall in long-term unemployment among younger males. Not all property crime is drug related. Many offenders become involved in crime simply because it provides a useful source of additional income. This is particularly true of burglary, which attracts a large number of casual opportunists. Studies show that young people from low socio-economic status families tend to commit property crime at a higher rate during periods of unemployment than when they have jobs. But to get back to drugs, it's worth noting that reducing the supply and increasing the cost of heroin is more likely to reduce crime when governments also ensure addicts are easily able to find a path out of drug use and into treatment.

CHAPTER 10
Our ageing population

When you start thinking about the ageing of the Australian population—how the proportion of people aged 65 or more is set to double over the next 40 years—it isn't hard to see problems. Politicians and bureaucrats tend to emphasise problems, partly because it's problems they're paid to fix, but also because they've found that engendering a crisis atmosphere is the way to get the public to accept unpopular changes. The media, too, almost invariably focus on problems. Why? Because they're in the business of selling news, and they've learnt that their customers much prefer buying bad news to good.

The terrible truth, however, is that the ageing of the population carries at least as much good news as bad. The proportion of older people in the population is rising for various reasons, but the greatest single reason is that we're living longer. Over the past

Our ageing population

century, life expectancy at birth has increased from 57 years to 80. And the population projections in the Productivity Commission's 2004 Draft Report on Ageing assume (conservatively) that, over the next 50 years, life expectancy will rise by a further six years.

This is something to feel bad about? It represents a historic human achievement, a triumph for public health officials, medical scientists, health workers of all types and even the odd economist. We've paid a pretty penny for this success, of course, but we do have a lot to show for it. And our lives aren't just longer, they're also much healthier. So that's the first point: population ageing is good news for everyone who prefers living to dying.

The second most important reason for the ageing of the population is the marked decline in the fertility rate (births per woman) since the early 1960s. I happen to think this is the worst part of the news. But I'm perfectly capable of giving it a positive spin. For one thing, having fewer children to support at least makes it easier for the community to support an increased number of old people. (Forget what this implies further down the track.) For another, it's possible fertility may be stabilising. It hasn't got any lower for six years. (Even if that's true, however, reduced fertility is good news for all those people who hate children and think there ought to be fewer of 'em.)

Next, ageing is great news for workers. The workforce will be growing much more slowly in coming years because fewer young people will be joining it and because the baby boomers will be reducing their participation in it—switching from full-time to part-time, for instance—as they approach and reach retirement. This means that, after enduring 30 years in which the supply of labour exceeded the demand for it, we're about to revert to the position that applied for the first 30 years after World War II, where the demand for labour exceeded its supply.

And that means the balance of bargaining power is going to shift from bosses back to workers. Unemployment will be much less of an issue, redundancies will be rare, older workers will be hung on to and their needs accommodated, and bosses will be trying a lot harder to keep their workers—even their unskilled workers—happy. In the post-war period, big businesses used various devices to bind their experienced workers to them. For instance, company super schemes worked in such a way that, the longer you'd been in the scheme, the more you had to lose by leaving before you reached retirement.

In recent times, companies have worked assiduously to weaken their ties to employees, moving to more part-time, contract and casual employment and reserving the right to lay off staff whenever the gods of the stockmarket needed to be propitiated. Partly to encourage greater 'labour mobility', governments have made superannuation portable between employers. Believe me, WorkChoices or no, it won't be long before employers revert to encouraging loyalty and rewarding long service. Why? Not because they've suddenly become nice guys, but because of the turnaround in market forces. They'll screw you if they can; they'll suck up to you if they must.

Because ageing means we'll see much slower growth in the total number of hours worked each year, this will mean much slower growth in the economy overall. The Productivity Commission estimates that, by the mid-2020s, the rate of growth in real income per person will have almost halved, to 1.25 per cent a year. This is the bit most economists regard as the really bad news. They're hooked on economic growth—growth in the economy's production of goods and services—and, to them, such a slowdown spells failure.

But here's the good news: it may worry the economists, but we know from the research into happiness that it won't much worry you and me. The economists prefer not to think about it, but studies show that in the rich countries, rising incomes don't lead to greater 'subjective wellbeing'. What people care about is not so much what's happening to their incomes in absolute terms, but what's happening in relative terms—how their pay rise compares with other people at work or their brother-in-law. Slower growth in incomes generally won't stop us playing these stupid status games.

But, to give it its due, the commission does point to other reasons why the slowdown in economic growth won't be as bad—or as great—as it appears.

First, because a higher proportion of the population will be retired, the population will be enjoying a lot more leisure. Gross domestic product (GDP) ignores leisure, but people enjoy it in retirement and often choose to retire voluntarily. Similarly, as measured by GDP, economic growth ignores volunteer work which, though unpaid, is highly beneficial to the community. The commission estimates that, thanks to the increase in retirees, the value of volunteer labour will increase over the next 40 years from 1.8 per cent of GDP to 2.2 per cent.

And there's good news for the young. Though they may be paying a bit more tax to support their oldies, their lifetime *real* incomes will be substantially higher—maybe 90 per cent higher—than their parents' lifetime incomes. And though their parents and grandparents have cleaned up in the real estate market, as we saw in Chapter 5, one way or another much of that wealth will eventually be passed on to them.

But whether population ageing is good news or bad—it's actually both—it will surely be one of the biggest factors reshaping our world in the years to come. And though politicians and bureaucrats have been talking about it for ages, I suspect a lot of us don't know as much about it as we think we do. For instance, any fool knows the problem's caused by the imminent retirement of the baby boomers. And a lot of business people know the solution to the problem is increased immigration. Wrong and wrong. Before we examine the economic and social implications of ageing in greater detail, let's get a clearer understanding of the underlying demographic causes and possible solutions. We can do so with the help of the Productivity Commission's draft report.

To have an ageing population means that an increasing *proportion* of the population is accounted for by older age groups. Consider this: 100 years ago, less than one Australian in 25 was aged 65 years or more. Today, it's one in every eight. In 40 year's time, 2044–45, it's projected to be one in four. The most common indicator of ageing is the 'aged dependency ratio'—the ratio of those aged 65 and over to those aged 15 to 64 (that is, those of standard working age). According to the Productivity Commission's projections (which are consistent with those used in the Howard Government's Intergenerational Report of 2002), the

Our ageing population

aged dependency ratio may rise from 19 per cent today to more than 44 per cent in 40 years' time.

In order of importance, the ageing of the population is a product of four factors: rising longevity, declining fertility, the progress of the baby boomers and the level of immigration. Starting with longevity, the rate at which people are dying has been falling and the average age to which they are living has been rising for well over a century. Much of this improvement stems from a decline in infant mortality but, more recently, adults are living longer because of the use of antibiotics to cure infectious diseases, and much more effective treatment of heart disease.

To demonstrate the contribution of increased life expectancy, the commission looked at what would have happened to the aged dependency rate had there been no further gain in longevity after World War II. It found that, rather than rising to 44 per cent in 2045, as is projected, the aged dependency rate would have risen only to about 23 per cent. In fact, the commission's projection assumes (in line with the Bureau of Statistics' middle projection, known as Series B) that, by 2051, life expectancy at birth will have risen by a further seven years for men and five for women.

Next, fertility. The 'total fertility rate'—the average number of births per woman—has varied a lot over the past century, falling to as low as 2.1 births when the Depression of the 1930s was at its worst, but in the post-war baby-boom period rising to a peak of 3.6 in 1961. Some people (though not the commission) take that year as the end of the baby boom because the fertility rate then fell rapidly during the 1960s and 1970s.

The fall has been more moderate since then and for the past six years has been steady at 1.76 births. This marked fall in fertility over the past 40 years is explained by the advent of the contraceptive pill, changes in the interpretation of abortion law, and marked increases in the education level and labour force participation of women.

Despite the apparent steadying of the fertility rate, the commission's projection assumes it will fall to 1.6 births per woman by 2011 and then stay constant. But the rise in the aged dependency ratio over the next 40 years will be influenced far more by the fall in fertility over the past 40 years than by what may or may not happen to fertility over the coming 40. By 2045, the absolute number of kids aged below 15 is projected to have fallen by 250 000—even though the total population is projected to have grown by 6.5 million.

Be clear on this: increasing longevity and declining fertility are the two dominant influences over population ageing. To demonstrate the lesser role played by the progress of the baby boomers—defined here as people born between 1946 and 1966, who will thus reach the standard retirement age between 2011 and 2031—the commission looked at what would have happened had there been no baby boom. It assumed the fertility rate recovered to just 2.5 in 1947 (rather than the actual 3) and then gradually declined to where it is today.

It found that, had there been no baby boom, population ageing would have started a lot earlier than it did, with the aged dependency rate higher than projected until the mid-2030s, and little different thereafter. So the main effect of the baby boom has been to *defer* population ageing and make its onset more pronounced. The rate at which people cross the line to 65 accelerates from now to 2015.

The last of the four demographic factors is immigration (strictly speaking, 'net migration'—immigration minus emigration). Following the Bureau of Statistics, the commission's projection assumes the level of net migration falls from its present 125 000 a year to 100 000 by 2005/06, and stays there until 2051. OK, so let's beef that up and see what difference it would make. Let's assume the level of net migration stays at 125 000 a year for the next 40 years. That would cause the proportion of the population aged 65 or more in 2045 to be not 26.1 per cent but 25.6 per cent. Wow. Some difference.

Well, let's be more ambitious. What would it take to delay (note that, merely delay) any increase in the aged dependency rate for the next 40 years? It would require a net migrant inflow equivalent to 3.35 per cent of the population each year for 40 years. We'd have to start with an intake of 660 000 a year and have it grow to 3.7 million people a year, by which time our total population would be not the 26.2 million we're projecting, but 114 million (no, it's not a misprint).

To do that, or anything remotely like it, is clearly impossible, for a host of reasons—not the least of which is that, because just about every other country has an ageing issue, the competition for immigrants will be fierce. The reason increased immigration would do so little to slow the ageing process is partly because migrants age too, but mainly because the longevity and fertility factors are so dominant.

With the basic demography sorted, now we can examine the economic and social implications. Politicians and bureaucrats have been rabbiting on about ageing for ages and in that time they've succeeded in giving the public one very clear impression: the big problem will be the immense pressure on the Federal Budget caused partly by the cost of health care for the aged, but mainly by the cost of the age pension. The impression was greatly reinforced by the Intergenerational Report, with its finding that ageing would cause the gap between government spending and revenue to blow out to 5 per cent of GDP (or about $50 billion a year in today's dollars over the following 40 years).

But get this: if you actually read the Intergenerational Report you discover the budgetary costs of ageing aren't nearly as great as most of us have gathered. It turns out that, of the much-trumpeted 5.3 percentage-point increase in government spending between now and 2042, fully 4.1 percentage points relate to increased federal spending on health care. Of that 4.1 points, 2.8 points come from the projected growth in the cost of just one program, the Pharmaceutical Benefits Scheme. And here's the thing: less than a third of the projected increase in health-care spending is related to the ageing of the population. All the rest is 'non-demographic', the result of projecting into the future the same rate of growth in health-care spending that we've experienced in the past 20 years or so.

What happened to the blowout in the cost of the age pension? Its share of GDP is projected to grow from 2.9 per cent to 4.6—a rise of 1.7 points. At the same time, the report projects that the share of GDP going on the disability support pension and the sole parent's pension will be unchanged over the next 40 years, while the share going to unemployment benefits will halve and the share going on family benefits will fall by 40 per cent. These savings cut the *overall* increase in pension and benefit payments to just 0.6 of a point.

There are two reasons we don't have the age pension problem all other developed countries have. One, our age pension is frugal, flat-rate and tightly means-tested. And two, the Hawke–Keating Government's introduction of compulsory superannuation in 1992. In 20 or 30 years' time, this will be significantly reducing (though rarely completely eliminating) individuals' eligibility for the age pension. There's a popular view that people had better start making provision for their own retirement because the cost of the age pension will grow so huge that the government will simply abandon it. It's codswallop. Grey Power will be such a dominant political force that no government would dare.

The next thing you realise if you actually read the report is that the 5.3 percentage-point budget blowout arises because government spending is allowed to grow, whereas revenue is held constant as a percentage of GDP. Get it? We've got a looming fiscal crisis—what on earth can we do about it? In a kind of glossy, kiddies' version of the Intergenerational Report issued in 2004, *Australia's Demographic Challenges*, we're told we face four choices: keep raising tax revenue as a proportion of GDP as necessary to prevent the budget going into deficit (say, by 5 per cent); slash government spending by 5 per cent of GDP; just accept the deficits and allow government debt to build up enormously; or look for ways to counter the expected slowdown in the economy's rate of growth so that it comes closer to keeping pace with the projected growth in government spending.

Now here's a test of how well you understand the economists' mindset: which of the four do you reckon we're supposed to choose? Well, raising taxes by 5 per cent of GDP would involve the equivalent of doubling the rate of the GST or increasing personal income-tax collections by more than 40 per cent. And cutting government spending by 5 per cent of GDP would be practically impossible. We'd have to either stop all spending on health care or halve our spending on social security. But moving the budget into permanent deficit, so that government debt was growing by up to 5 per cent of GDP *per year*, would be utterly unsustainable.

Clever you—you guessed it! The only remotely attractive answer is to pull out all the stops to make the economy grow faster. And I hope by now you've got the commercial message from the economic rationalists as to how that could be done: by seeking to counter the expected decline in the proportion of the population participating in the labour force and by using more micro-economic reform to boost the growth in the productivity of labour. Conventional economists specialise in identifying ways to quicken the growth in GDP—our production of goods and services. It's the only product they've got to sell, and boy do they sell it. Faster economic growth is the answer to all problems, even damage to the environment.

But while the economists believe they're doing us a great favour in whipping us on to ever-increasing production and consumption of goods and services—they're the high priests in the Temple of Mammon—we need to think harder about their assumption that a

Our ageing population

rise in tax revenue as a proportion of GDP would be unthinkable. In truth, it makes a lot of sense and, in reality, it's likely to be the main way the growth in government spending *is* covered.

For a start, what's so inviolable about the present level of federal taxes—roughly 27 per cent of GDP? Why draw a line in the sand at this exact point and tell ourselves it would be a disaster to cross it? For federal taxes to go no higher as a proportion of GDP would require a degree of restraint of bracket creep that neither the Howard Government nor any before it has managed to impose on themselves. The proportion of taxes to GDP has been creeping up for decades. Why? Because the public sector has been progressively delivering to us more and better services.

When you think about it, the prospect of annual income-tax collections growing by 40 per cent over the next 40 years isn't all that frightening. And don't forget the economic scenario on which all these figures are based implies that real output per worker *doubles* over the 40 years. Professors Steve Dowrick and Peter McDonald of the Australian National University calculate that, if taxes were held constant as a percentage of GDP, real after-tax incomes in 2042 would be 100 per cent higher than they are today. Were the tax proportion allowed to rise, however, the growth in real after-tax incomes would be a mere 85 per cent. Really? Frightening!

And when you remember how much of the growth in government spending is expected to come from increased spending on health care, what you're implying by trying to hold down the tax proportion is that it's a bad thing for us to devote a higher proportion of our incomes to health care as we get richer. Either that, or it's a bad thing for so much of our health-care spending to go via the public sector and such hugely cost-saving arrangements as the Pharmaceutical Benefits Scheme (which stops us being exploited by drug companies the way the Americans and Europeans are).

No, if you're searching for the really major economic and social implications of ageing, you won't find they reside in the budget. You'll find them in the jobs market and the world of work. And I suspect we'll be feeling them much sooner than most people realise. Peter Costello keeps talking about 'the demographic time bomb that's going to hit us in 20 years' time'. But that view is quite mistaken—as I'm sure Mr Costello would find if he checked his briefing notes.

Ageing isn't in the never-never, ageing is now. It isn't an event that will happen one day, it's a process—one that began more than 40 years ago. It's built up to the point where it will become quite noticeable within the next few years. The ageing process is speeding up and its effect on the labour market is now evident even over the course of a year. Over the 12 months to June 2004, the population as a whole grew by 1.2 per cent. Within that, however, the number of children aged up to 14 actually fell by 600, whereas the number of people aged 65 or more rose by 2.3 per cent. As a result, the nation's median age—the thing that's ageing—advanced by almost 2.5 months to 36.4 years. The population of working age—those aged 15 to 64—grew by 1.4 per cent. But within that, the population of pre-retirement age—55 to 64—grew by 4 per cent to 2.1 million.

In 1980, kids turning 18 constituted 1.8 per cent of the population. Today, it's 1.4 per cent. From 2010, just four years

Our ageing population

away, the number of 18-year-olds is projected to start falling. Now do you see what's happening? The fertility rate has been falling since 1961, while life expectancy has been rising for well over a century. These trends are inexorable, but slow. What gives the ageing process its urgency and bite is the progress of the bulge in the population python that's the baby boomers.

If you define the baby boom narrowly to cover those babies born in the first 16 years after World War II—from 1946 to 1961—there are now 4.4 million of these blighters, representing 22 per cent of the population. The boomers started reaching the minimum retirement age of 55 (the age when the federal government will let you get your hands on your super) in 2001. By now, about a third are 55 or older. The boomers start turning 60 in 2006. And guess what? The average retirement age is 60 for men and 58 for women.

Still think the demographic time bomb will hit in 20 years' time? Mr Costello's own budget in 2005 contained two clear indications that the first noticeable effects of ageing are almost upon us. The first was a prediction that the rate of participation in the labour force—the proportion of people of working age who either have a job or are looking for one—would reach its zenith in the next financial year, 2006/07. The second was the decision to cut the nation's projected potential rate of economic growth from 3.5 per cent a year to 3.25 per cent from 2008/09 onward. That slowdown in growth may seem minor, but it isn't. What's more, it will be the first of many. It flowed from a projection that the annual growth in total employment will slow from 1.5 per cent to 1.25 per cent—equivalent to the absence of about 27000 new workers a year.

While some people are happily imagining the time bomb won't hit for 20 years, various professions and industries are already studying the likely effects of the baby boomers' retirement. One study of the medical workforce was published by Deborah Schofield and John Beard of the University of Sydney. Defining baby boomers more broadly as those born between 1946 and 1964 they found that, in 2001, boomers accounted for 55 per cent of GPs, more than 60 per cent of nurses and about 60 per cent of specialists. Few nurses remain working after the age of 60. As doctors get older they tend to work fewer hours, even if they don't retire. And note this: Generation X doctors—those born from 1965 to 1974—tend to work fewer hours than the baby boomers did at the same age. 'It is widely anticipated that retirement among ageing clinicians will result in workforce shortages within the next five years,' Schofield and Beard say.

Turning to the nation's teachers, in 2001 Schofield and Beard found that 9 per cent of them were 55 or older (indicating that teachers tend to retire early), while a further third were aged 45 to 54. In the manufacturing industry, 170 000 skilled workers are expected to leave the industry in the next five years, which is 34 000 a year, compared with about 21 000 young people completing apprenticeships each year.

Looking more broadly, it gets down to the changing balance between the demand and supply of labour. Over the course of the 1970s, the total population (representing the demand for labour) grew by 14 per cent, whereas the population of working age (representing the potential supply of labour) grew by 18 per cent. It was a similar story of supply exceeding demand in the 1980s. By

Our ageing population

now, however, the gap between the two has narrowed. Over the first half of the noughties, population growth slowed to 6 per cent and growth in the working-age population to 7 per cent. For the rest of the noughties the gap between the two is projected to fall to just 0.5 percentage points. And from 2010 demand for labour is projected to outstrip supply—totalling a shortfall of potential supply of 2 percentage points during the 2010s.

We're not far from the time when shortages of labour are popping up everywhere. Do you see what this will do to enhance the bargaining power of workers? And it will be happening not long after John Howard's industrial relations changes have sought to shift bargaining power in favour of employers. Seems to me that the ageing of the population carries at least as much good news as bad.

PART THREE

EVERYDAY LIFE

CHAPTER 11
Housework has value

As girls have taken to education and, in consequence, as mothers they've returned to paid employment sooner or later after childbirth, the formerly mundane matter of housework has become more interesting and a lot more contentious. Are husbands doing their fair share? To what extent are modern appliances reducing the time busy people devote to housework? Then there's the growing tendency to bring paid workers into the home to help. Are we regressing to the age of the domestic servant, or providing job opportunities for the unskilled? And what's the economic significance of all this housework—how does all the unpaid work we do compare with our paid work?

Starting with the vexed question of who does how much and what around the house, I unearthed the definitive study. The results may surprise you—and their twists and turns certainly help explain why there's so much room for argument on this issue. The study, 'The Rush Hour', was undertaken by Professor Judy Wajcman of the Australian National University and Michael Bittman, formerly of the University of New South Wales's Social Policy Research Centre. It analyses the findings of the Bureau of Statistics' time-use survey of 1992, in which a large sample of people kept detailed diaries of the way they used their time. It focuses on the *average* time use for all men and women aged 20 to 59.

It's reasonable to assume things haven't changed greatly since 1992. If so, the first finding is that, yes, women do do more of the unpaid work around the house—housework, child care and shopping—than men. In fact, on average they do 77 per cent of it. This is pretty much par for the course among nine other OECD countries, though men's share of the housework gets as high as 30 per cent in Sweden and as low as 12 per cent in Italy.

The second finding, however, is that men do more *paid* work than women. Quite a bit more, in fact. So much so that, when you combine paid and unpaid work, you find that men and women do virtually the same amount—about 50 hours a week. If anything, men average 25 minutes a week more. Again, this result is very close to the OECD average—although, in Holland, men do almost three hours a week more 'total work' than women. Guess where the women do almost five hours a week more than men? Italy.

The next finding is that, since men and women do virtually the same amount of work and people spend the same amount of time on self-care (sleeping, eating, washing and dressing) regardless of gender, men and women also have virtually the same amount of free time, or leisure. About 36 hours a week each. So much for women's 'double shift'—perhaps.

At this point, however, the study takes what is for men a disturbing turn. If you switch from looking at the quantity of leisure to looking at its quality, you find big differences between the sexes. We know that, the pace of life being what it is, people are often doing two things at once. They may be ironing while watching television, for instance. The official time-use survey took account of this, asking people to nominate their primary activity and their secondary activity (if any) during the same period.

It turns out that, while men and women have the same amount of leisure, a much higher proportion of men's leisure is 'pure' leisure— it's not accompanied by any other activity. On average, men enjoy three hours a week more pure leisure than women do. Conversely, a higher proportion of women's leisure time is 'contaminated' by being combined with unpaid work, such as child-minding. Another difference is that, although their total hours of leisure are the same as men's, women have more *episodes* of leisure in the average day. And their maximum period of unbroken leisure time is shorter. In other words, women's leisure is more frequently interrupted.

'The fragmentary character of women's leisure lowers its quality,' the authors say. 'Fragmented leisure, snatched between work and self-care activities, is less relaxing than unbroken leisure. It's likely that this fragmented leisure will be experienced as more rushed and therefore increase self-reported stress. Indeed, it may well be that the contemporary view of increased "time pressure" has more to do with this fragmentation than with any measurable reduction in primary leisure time.'

GITTINOMIC$

Yet another difference between the sexes is that men enjoy more 'adult leisure'—leisure time without children present. For the adult population overall, men get almost four hours a week more adult leisure than women. The greater gulf, however, is not between the sexes but between those parents with young children and those without. Men and women with no children get eight times the amount of adult leisure that couples do whose youngest child is under 2. Among such couples, however, the husband gets three times the adult leisure the mother gets, which is two hours and 40 minutes a week.

When their youngest child is under 2, mothers devote an average of over 30 hours a week to primary, direct child care. More than half this time is spent on physical care—carrying, comforting, feeding, changing, dressing and bathing. Less than a sixth of it is spent playing with those kids.

By contrast, the fathers average eight hours a week child care, of which almost a third is devoted to play. So men experience children as an opportunity to play, while women are more likely to experience children as the occasion for unpaid work. Clearly, the *quality* of women's leisure time falls far short of men's. 'When the characteristics of the leisure are considered,' the authors conclude, 'the apparent equity in leisure time between men and women disappears.' Sorry to dob you in, chaps.

But the time devoted to housework would be a lot worse if it wasn't for all the labour-saving appliances we use these days, right? Well, no. Not according to more recent research by Wajcman and Bittman with James Rice of the Social Policy Research Centre at the University of New South Wales. According to the Bureau of Statistics' 1997 survey of time use, 83 per cent of people lived in a household with a microwave oven. For other appliances the proportions were 53 per cent with a freezer, 34 per cent with a dishwasher, 57 per cent with a clothesdryer and 76 per cent with a lawnmower or whipper-snipper.

Because access to this equipment was far from universal, it was possible to compare the time spent on chores by people who had them and people who didn't. The researchers found that, even though microwaves cook food very much faster than conventional stoves, women who have a microwave don't spend any less time on food preparation. Similarly, even though a freezer allows you to gain economies of scale by pre-cooking food in batches, women with freezers don't devote less time to food preparation.

There's no sign that possession of a dishwasher reduces the time women spend cleaning up after meals. But get this: women with clothesdryers spend about 20 minutes a week extra dealing with laundry. And men who own a lawnmower or whipper-snipper average about an hour a week longer on grounds care than those who don't. (If by now I've got your feminist hackles rising, note another finding of the research: there's no sign that the spread of time-saving appliances leads to any significant change in traditional gender division of household tasks.)

So owning domestic technology rarely reduces unpaid housework—and in some cases it actually increases the time spent on the relevant activity. How could this be possible? Well, the researchers can only speculate. But it seems likely that, as we become able to perform these tasks more quickly and easily, our standards rise. That is, we increase the quantity or quality of domestic production—for example, more or better meals, cleaner clothes or more attractive gardens.

In other words, we've used the appliances to increase output rather than to save time. That increased output represents an improvement in our material standard of living, of course. It's just that this improvement occurs so gradually we're hardly conscious of it. All we know is that we're doing as much housework as ever.

Unfortunately, we don't have measures of the quantity (let alone the quality) of the output from domestic labour. So it's not possible to prove this theory. But there is some supporting evidence. When we look at household incomes, we see two things. Not surprisingly, we see that households with higher incomes tend to have more labour-saving appliances. But we also see that large differences in income produce only small changes in the amount of time devoted to housework. This suggests that higher-income households use their appliances (and any paid household help) to produce a higher output of goods and services—to maintain larger, more refined and more pleasant homes.

Speaking of paid help around the house, it could make you think that the trend for big businesses to 'outsource' their 'non-core activities' to other firms had spread to the home. With 57 per cent of married women now in paid employment—more two-income families than ever—more of us have become 'income rich, but time poor'. Thus many of us, it is believed, are paying for the performance of various kinds of housework that formerly we did ourselves. As part of this, we're bringing people into our homes to act as cleaners, child-minders or nannies, people to do our washing and ironing, people to mow our lawns and do gardening.

Housework has value

But is this a healthy social trend? Attitudes differ. Some commentators see it as the re-emergence of something we confidently believed was dead and gone forever: domestic service. Is the servant making a comeback in supposedly egalitarian Australia? Some US observers see in this not just a strengthening of class barriers, but overtones of racial and ethnic dominance—here in America, they say, rich white families are employing and possibly exploiting poor immigrant women with bad English and dubious migration status. Is it all that different in Australia? Are our cleaners and nannies all getting proper breaks and award wages? And what about our kids? Are we regressing to the *Upstairs, Downstairs* world where children are deprived of intimate contact with their preoccupied parents?

Standing against these gloomy sentiments, however, are the economic optimists. All we're witnessing, they say, is the latest stage in the long-standing process of economic development. Tasks have been shifting from the home to the market for centuries; this is just the new frontier. Phil Ruthven, the forecaster from IBIS Business Information, put it nicely: in the agrarian revolution we outsourced the *growing* of things, in the industrial revolution we outsourced the *making* of things and now, in the infotronics revolution, we're outsourcing the *doing* of things.

In any case, where's the problem? We have a rise in the number of highly paid managers and professionals—women as well as men—but their incomes are being recycled to the less skilled—particularly women—via the outsourcing of domestic tasks. But, as the *Australian Financial Review* saw it in an editorial in 1998, many busy middle-class families can't afford the high wages paid to domestic servants and many Australians don't want to do such work.

So why don't we do what many countries have done and introduce a program of 'guest workers'? Live-in maids in Indonesia are commonly paid as little as $40 a month. Many young women from Asia would leap at the chance to come here for a few years, earning, say, $5200 a year plus superior food and accommodation. They'd be better off, their families back home would be better off and so would many time-pressed Australian families.

So what's it to be: is the outsourcing of housework a bane or a boon? Try none of the above. It's fun to build grand theories on our casual observation of changes in the world around us, but it's always a good idea to touch base with the facts. This is just what Michael Bittman and his fellow workers at the Social Policy Research Centre in the University of New South Wales did in another study. Every few years the Bureau of Statistics conducts a survey of exactly what households spend their money on. Bittman compared the household expenditure surveys for 1984 and 1998 to determine just what changes have occurred in household outsourcing.

His results may surprise you. Let's start with cleaning, the area that's attracted the most adverse comment. The most recent figures show that a mere 3 per cent of households paid for cleaning services. And there was no significant change in this over the previous 14 years. (Nor does it follow that most of those who do pay for cleaning are employing particular women, as opposed to using contract cleaners who whip through many houses each week and see themselves as small business people, not servants.)

Housework has value

Next, paid lawnmowing and gardening. This grew somewhat over the decade to 1994, but still applied to only 9 per cent of households. Then there's laundry. Ten per cent of households out-sourced clothes care by making use of drycleaning and laundry services, but this spending actually declined over the decade. We're sending laundry out less today than we were before World War II. Presumably we're less fussy about starching and ironing things, and we're making more use of 'mod cons' such as automatic washing machines and clothesdryers.

One area where we *have* been doing more outsourcing is, not surprisingly, child care. Spending on child care has grown strongly and, by 1998, one-third of households with children under 15 were doing it. (Bear in mind that the Hawke–Keating government greatly increased spending on the provision of subsidised child care.) The incidence of such spending rises with income. About a quarter of the poorest of families were paying, compared with 40 per cent of the high-income families.

But almost all the growth was in spending on institutional care (child-minding centres, creches, kindergartens and pre-schools) with little growth in spending on baby-sitters and child-minders. As for nannies, the modest amounts spent on non-institutional care imply that less than 1 per cent of families could be running to the expense of a nanny.

And as for all those neglected children, separate time-use surveys show that, between 1987 and 1992, both men's and women's time devoted to primary face-to-face child care grew modestly. So more spending on paid care did not replace unpaid care by parents (though it may have reduced unpaid care by relations and friends). This continues what seems to be a century-long trend of Australians devoting both more time and more money to our kids, even while family size has fallen. We should feel guilty?

But the area where there was most replacement of house-work by paid services was food preparation. In the two weeks of the 1994 survey, 90 per cent of households spent money on restaurant meals, take-aways or school lunches, spending which had grown significantly over the previous decade. Spending on these things rises with the household's income, but those that can't afford to eat out often at least can afford take-aways. As well, the proportion of grocery spending going on raw food (such as flour, cereals, vegetables and meat) declined in favour of reduced-preparation foods (pasta sauces, pizza bases) and convenience foods (processed meat, biscuits, confectionery and fruit).

It would be a big mistake to conclude from all this that house-work was a relatively insignificant part of social and economic life. Far from it. Pioneering work undertaken by Dr Duncan Ironmonger at Melbourne University's Households Research Unit reveals that the 'household economy' accounts for a huge chunk of the economy overall. Conventional economics has tended to underestimate the role that households play in the economy. In theory, economics is concerned with all forms of work and production, but in practice it has limited itself to those forms of work and production that are provided in exchange for money (thus allowing their value to be determined easily). Households' role in the economy has been seen merely as providing labour to

Housework has value

the market economy, then consuming the goods and services it produces.

When you think about it, however, it's obvious that much unpaid work is carried out in households, that this work produces goods and services consumed by households, and that many of the goods and services households purchase from the market economy aren't consumed directly, but rather are used as 'inputs' to the household production process. Looking at it this way, you can see that The Economy consists of two parts, a 'market economy' where everything is exchanged for money, plus a 'household economy' where much the same processes occur without the use of money. What's more, the market economy and the household economy are, to some extent, in competition. We can make our own meals, or buy them in restaurants; we can clean our clothes and homes, maintain our gardens and houses, mind our children—or we can pay someone to do it for us.

Economists know a lot about the market economy but surprisingly little about the household economy. How important is it? How does it compare in size to the market economy? How does it work? These are questions that Dr Ironmonger and his team set out to answer. They've been able to begin finding answers thanks to several surveys of the uses of time in households conducted by the Bureau of Statistics.

Dr Ironmonger estimates that in 2000, we did about 382 million hours of unpaid household work each week. This compared with 321 million hours a week of work by people in paid employment. So we actually do more unpaid work than paid work. And this seems to be true in most developed countries. Not surprisingly,

183

men do more of the paid work than women do. And women do much more of the unpaid work. But, as we've seen, when you combine the paid and unpaid work, men and women do pretty much the same amount of work each week. Since 1974, the total amount of work has grown at pretty much the same rate as the population aged 15 and over. But unpaid work has grown at a faster rate than paid work.

The next step in estimating the monetary size of the household economy is to put a value on all this unpaid work. There are various ways to do this—you could value all the hours at the going wage rate for a housekeeper, or you could value each type of work at the wage rate paid to people who perform such work in the market economy—but Dr Ironmonger has used simply the average wage or salary rate (including fringe benefits) paid to workers in the market economy. For 2000 this was $19.26 an hour.

This put the value of unpaid work performed in 2000 at $383 billion. But to calculate the total value added by the household economy—'Gross Household Product' (GHP), as Dr Ironmonger calls it—we need to add the contribution made by capital. He puts this at about $36 billion from the use of household equipment and vehicles and $52 billion from the use of owner-occupied housing. So GHP was $471 billion, which was not a whole lot smaller than 'Gross Market Product' (essentially, conventional GDP) in the same year of $604 billion. Putting it another way, the total value of goods and services produced either by the market economy or the household economy ('Gross Economic Product') was $1075 billion, with the household economy accounting for 44 per cent of total production.

Housework has value

According to Dr Ironmonger's way of looking at it, the household economy consists of seven separate but related industries covering the preparation of meals, laundry and house-cleaning, child care, shopping, repairs and maintenance, gardening, and other household tasks. If you measure the size of industries by the number of hours of work expended in them, the three largest industries in the economy aren't in the market economy, but in the household economy: child care; preparation of meals, laundry and house-cleaning; and shopping. Each of these activities absorbs about 70 million hours a week of work, compared with the four largest market industries: wholesale and retail trade (58 million hours a week), community services (health and education, 46 million hours), manufacturing (44 million) and finance and business services (43 million).

Let's take a closer look at what Dr Ironmonger regards as the largest industry in the economy, the 'household restaurant and fast food industry'. This industry has more than 8 million kitchens, many of which contain the latest equipment and have been modenised in the renovation boom of the 1980s. In 1997, the labour required was almost twice the labour required in Australia's manufacturing industry. Women did almost three-quarters of the preparation, serving, clearing of tables and washing of dishes. By 2005, the proportion of households with electric or gas cooking equipment and refrigerators was virtually 100 per cent. According to Roy Morgan single source data, 59 per cent of households had freezers and 41 per cent had dishwashers. Between 1983 and 2005, the proportion of households with microwave ovens rose from 10 per cent to 84 per cent.

'This diffusion of kitchen technology to almost saturation took place in the 1960s and 1970s and can be expected to have led to substantial saving in the time involved in meal preparation, to a reduction in food wastage and to an improvement in the quality of meals served in Australian households', Dr Ironmonger wrote. Competition for the industry comes from the commercial sector, which comprises restaurants, cafes, hotels, motels, clubs, fast-food shops and take-away outlets. These establishments sell 92 million main meals, light meals and snacks a week. Households provide about 470 million main meals, light meals and snacks a week. So, in spite of the strong growth of the commercial fast-food and restaurant industry, in 2004 more than 80 per cent of all meals were prepared and served at home.

There are significant economies of scale in the household meal preparation industry. To cook for four takes only a little more time than to cook for two. Using the inflation rate to update figures Dr Ironmonger calculated for 1987, the cost of household-provided meals (including labour cost) for households with two adults is $23 per adult per day. Using this figure, we can estimate the additional cost of meals in households with children is less than $6 per child per day.

Well, treating households as though they were industries and taking unpaid work as seriously as paid work is certainly good fun, but does it have a more serious purpose? It does to Dr Ironmonger and his associates. 'Debunking the myth that "work" and "production" take place only in the market is critical both to women whose domestic labour remains unrecognised and unaccounted for, and for economists and social policy-makers who currently view the world with one eye closed,' he says. All policy areas need to recognise that unpaid work is valuable.

CHAPTER 12
The pleasures of consumerism

I don't suppose there are many who'd doubt we live in a consumerist society. But I doubt if many of us realise just how hooked on consumption we've become. Consider our attitude to money. We see our problem as not having enough of it, whereas you can argue that we've long had far more than we really need. In his book *Growth Fetish*, Clive Hamilton quotes the result of an opinion poll his Australia Institute commissioned in 2002, where 62 per cent of respondents believed they couldn't afford to buy everything they really needed. And 56 per cent said they spent nearly all their money on the basic necessities of life.

Really? As Dr Hamilton points out, Australia's real income per person has increased by more than half in just the past 20 years. That is, after allowing for inflation, income per person

The pleasures of consumerism

has gone from $27 800 a year in 1984–85 to $42 500 a year in 2004–05. (It's doubled since 1967 and trebled since 1950.) So whereas we see ourselves as struggling to keep up and pay the bills, Hamilton says the great majority of us were comfortable enough in the early 1980s, and now we're 55 per cent richer than we were then. He thinks we're all a bit like Kerry Packer was, wondering where to spend his next million. We've spent the past 20 years trying to think of ways to spend all the surplus income that's come our way.

I'll bet you've never thought of your family finances like that before. We focus on all the things we can't afford, whereas Hamilton focuses on all the things we *have* afforded. And when you think about it that way, you realise there's something in what he says. Certainly, we haven't really been spending all that extra income on 'the basic necessities of life'. Top of my list of what we've been doing with our increased wealth is spending it on bigger and better houses. The average floor size of a new house has increased by about a third just since 1986.

Second on my list would be cars. It never ceases to amaze me the money we pour into cars. We buy more of them—getting on for half of all households have two or more cars—and they're a lot fancier than they were. How many of us pay far more for an imported European car that performs little better than a locally made Toyota? And what about the proliferation of those huge four-wheel-drives that never leave the bitumen? Linking houses and cars is air-conditioning. We added it to our cars and now we're doing our homes. The annual peak in electricity consumption used to be on a cold winter's night, when everyone was home cooking dinner with the lights and heaters on. Now, because of the spread of air-conditioning, the peak is on a hot summer's day.

As our incomes have risen, the number of children we're having has fallen. But that leaves us with more money to lavish on our kids. 'Despite the availability of free education, large numbers of households with no more than average incomes choose to outlay tens of thousands of dollars to send their children to private schools', Dr Hamilton writes. After the money we lavish on kids comes the money we lavish on pets. Don't tell your friends you've just spent $400 at the vet's prolonging your elderly dog's life unless you want to be effortlessly topped by someone who's spent $1000 or more.

Then there's leisure. Recreation used to be something you did—now it's something you buy. We used to attend football matches; now we get a much better and more comfortable view watching at home on wide-screen television. These days, most entertainment comes in expensive electronic machines. We even go out and buy things just for the fleeting entertainment shopping brings. (I don't suppose I should put the growing sums we're spending on cosmetic surgery under the heading of 'leisure'—nor all the money we flush down the toilet after swallowing overpriced 'alternative medicines'.)

There's more, but I'll stop with all the money we spend making ourselves fatter. It's not just the fast food and quietly increasing size of portions. There's all the money we've spent over many decades taking the exercise out of paid work, housework and leisure. And now, as we realise what this is doing to our bodies, there's all the money we're spending trying to put the exercise back into our lives. There are the expensive gym memberships (plus appropriate footwear and clothing). There are the electronic treadmills, exercise bikes and rowing machines we prefer to doing the real thing out of doors.

But if the truth is that we're pouring much of our extra income into stuff we don't really need and oftentimes doesn't do us any good, how come we usually see the process so differently? Because we're hooked on the false promise of materialism—the next dollar we spend will be the one that finally makes us happy—and because, as herd animals, we're possessed by the need to fit in and, if possible, get to the front of the herd. Modern capitalists play on our weaknesses to keep their sales and profits eternally growing. But don't be angry—in their own way they're just as hooked as we are.

A strange thing about economists is that, although their ministrations exalt consumption above all things, they show remarkably little interest in it. They're obsessed by maximising it, but uninterested in studying it. As we'll see in this chapter, most of what's worth knowing about consumption comes from psychologists (plus a few tell-tale marketers). But one subject on which economists do have something useful to say is the widespread practice of 'price discrimination'.

Consider Capitalists' Heaven. What would be the ideal world from the point of view of a business person trying to make as much money as possible? It would be a world where he or she could charge each customer a different price, that price being the maximum the particular customer was prepared to pay. Fortunately for customers, it's not possible for business people to run their businesses that way, much as they'd like to. The problem isn't the high administrative cost of charging so many different prices, it's that the business person has no way of knowing how much each individual is prepared to pay.

Charging every individual the maximum price he or she was prepared to pay would be the ultimate form of price discrimination. The price discrimination we get in practice usually involves setting only a few different prices, not thousands. But the principle is the same: businesses charge different prices to different classes of customer because it's the best way they can find to maximise their profits.

Take airlines, for instance. They divide their customers into two basic classes—business travellers and holiday travellers. Business travellers usually have a more pressing reason for wanting to make the trip and their fares, being a business expense, are tax deductible. Holiday-makers, on the other hand, have a limited amount to spend, don't get a tax deduction and often have ankle-biters in tow.

The airlines want to carry both groups, of course, but they'd also like to be able to charge business travellers a higher price than they could get away with charging holiday-makers, who won't make the trip if the price is too high. How do they do it? By introducing such things as earlybird fares for holiday-makers so they can raise their standard fares—which then apply mainly to business travellers. The conditions attached to earlybird fares— including a minimum number of nights' stay—are designed to ensure they go only to holiday-makers.

But earlybird fares are just the start of the price discrimination practised by the airlines. Their first class and business class fares are a device for discriminating *between* business travellers. In

The pleasures of consumerism

other words, the premium they're able to charge for first class and business class seats is a lot greater than the extra cost to the airline of the bigger seats and better service.

But it's not just the airlines. A lot more price discrimination goes on than you probably realise. Why, for instance, do cinemas and other places of entertainment charge half price for children? Why do they offer concession prices for students and pensioners? Why do some hairdressers charge pensioners less on Wednesday afternoons? Answer: not because they're nice guys, but because they've discovered it's the best way to maximise their profits. In each of these cases, the quantity and quality of the service provided at a discount price is identical to that being provided to people who pay the full price. So how can it be more profitable, rather than less, to charge some customers less than others? Well, it gets back to our profit-maximising ideal, which is to charge each individual the maximum—but not a cent more than the maximum—he or she is prepared to pay.

As a generalisation, parents aren't prepared to pay a lot for their kids to go to the movies because it gets too expensive. Similarly, students and pensioners aren't prepared to pay as much as working adults are. If it's too expensive they'll go without. If theatre-owners charged only a single admission price, it would have to be lower than their current adult price if they wanted to attract enough children, students and pensioners to maximise their total attendances. But if they charge a special, lower price for children, they're able to get lots of kids along while raising the price they charge adults beyond what they could charge if they had only a single price.

These calculations are based on the assumption that the theatre-owner has plenty of spare seats he'd like to fill. The cost to the owner of admitting an extra person is tiny, so he's better off even if the price he charges the extra person is a lot smaller than the price he's charging other members of the audience. Of course, there are other occasions—such as the football finals or a popular live theatre performance—when the organisers know they can easily fill all the seats. In such cases they *would* be losing money if they offered half-price seats for kids—which is why they don't. And that, in fact, is the proof that businesses charge lower prices for children, students and pensioners so as to maximise their profits, not because they are nice guys or even because they're bound by some social convention.

Quantity discounts, the generic no-frills products sold in supermarkets, department stores' end-of-season clothing sales, the 'honeymoon rates' banks charge new home-loan customers, the higher prices farmers and manufacturers charge their local customers as opposed to their export customers—all these are further examples of price discrimination. It's not always possible for businesses to engage in price discrimination, however. There have to be differences in your customers' willingness to pay, you have to be able to prevent your low-price customers re-selling to your high-price customers and there has to be an absence of competitors willing to undercut your high prices.

Our steadily rising living standards over the years have been accompanied by an expanding array of things to choose from. At least since Bob Menzies' day, the Liberal Party has sung the praises of Choice. More recently, economic rationalists are always citing

The pleasures of consumerism

Increased Choice as one of the great benefits of the competition they're promoting. Having a wider range to pick from is supposed to be a benefit in itself, quite apart from lower prices or improvements in quality. But though some choice is obviously better than none, I think choice isn't all it's cracked up to be. In fact, I'm starting to think choice is one of the great cons of consumer capitalism. It's supposed to be a benefit to consumers, but more often it's a benefit to business.

For a start, consumers often find the choices they're presented with quite confusing. You're being asked to compare an apple with an orange. One bank offers you a loan with no up-front fees, whereas another has a $750 'establishment fee' but its interest rate is 0.25 percentage points lower. Which is better? (Answer: don't try to work it out unless you have an intimate familiarity with discounted cash flow analysis.)

Psychologists tell us our brains are simply not capable of making rational choices between more than two options with differing features. Consider this experiment involving someone choosing a flat to rent. To oversimplify reality, the person has only two concerns: the amount of the rent and the flat's distance from their workplace. Flat A is very expensive, but wonderfully close to work. Flat B is the opposite: a long way from work, but very cheap. So which is better? It's not really possible to judge, so people tend to divide between them pretty much 50/50. But now add Flat C, which is near B but both more expensive and further out. Now, more than 70 per cent of people pick B. See how our reasoning processes fail us? C is clearly worse than B, so it's irrelevant to the real but tricky choice between A and B. Because the choice between B and C is so easy, however, it diverts our attention and misleads us into favouring B over A when there's no sensible reason to do so.

It follows from this that, in their pursuit of higher sales and profits, businesses often use choice to manipulate their customers. A real estate salesperson, for instance, will usually show you cheaper but nastier properties before they take you to the ones they think you'll like. Why? They're softening you up to pay a higher price. The phone companies' arrays of mobile phone 'plans' are horrendously complicated and hard to compare. I can't believe this is accidental.

Often we're offered a choice between an ordinary product and a dearer one with more features. Examples include private health insurance plans with and without 'extras', and the choice between a 'standard' variable home loan or a no–frills 'basic' loan (the interest rate on which is 0.55 percentage points lower). But when you study these 'choices' carefully (or talk to an insider), you find the cheaper version has pretty much all the features you're likely to use, whereas the dearer version has extra features you're unlikely to use (such as, in the case of health insurance extras, home nursing). The dearer version is there to exploit people with unrealistic expectations about what they may do in the future, or just those with more money than sense (in the home-loan case, those who think of themselves as 'standard' people, a cut above 'basic' people).

Shops selling fast food on the basis of quantity usually know better than to offer a choice of large or small. Small is for cheapskates, large is for gutses. People will hesitate at the counter for ages choosing between those unattractive options. But offer the popcorn–at–the–movies choice of three—large, medium or small—

and most people will quickly choose medium. Most of us are happy to think of ourselves as middle of the road. Another widely used choice of three is between deluxe, regular and economy. That range offers most people what they need to gratify their image of themselves. Economy is for people (particularly women) who pride themselves on being price-conscious, canny shoppers. Deluxe is for people (particularly men) who like to think they 'always buy the best'. Being neither tacky nor flashy, regular is for people with 'good taste'. With things like cars—or houses—we often select the model not so much for its intrinsic characteristics as for its ability to demonstrate to the world our success and social status.

There's often intense rivalry between the handful of big companies in an industry, but they usually choose to compete on choice and marketing rather than price—because a price war would benefit only the customer.

All my scepticism about the virtues of choice is confirmed by psychologist Barry Schwartz in his book, *The Paradox of Choice*. Dr Schwartz, a professor of psychology at Swarthmore College in Philadelphia, accepts that a degree of choice improves the quality of our lives. It's essential to our autonomy—which is fundamental to our wellbeing—allowing us to direct our own lives and express our individuality. What doesn't follow, however, is that if *some* choice is good, *more* choice must be better. Dr Schwartz argues that too much choice contributes to bad decisions, anxiety, stress and dissatisfaction.

The first point is that we don't actually like having a lot of choices. Consider this experiment. Researchers set up a display of exotic, high-quality jams in a gourmet food store. In one case they allowed people to taste 24 varieties. In another case they offered tastes of just six varieties even though they still had 24 on sale. In both cases they gave people a dollar off if they bought a jar. The larger array of jams attracted more people to the table, though in each case people tasted about the same number of jams. But here's the trick: 30 per cent of the people exposed to the small array of jams actually bought a jar; only 3 per cent of those exposed to the large array did so.

The next point is that, as we saw with the experiment about choosing a flat, people aren't particularly good at making choices, and adding options can confuse them. Imagine you're in the market for a new music system and see a sign in a shop window announcing a one-day clearance sale of CD players. You can get a popular Sony CD player for only $99, well below list price. Do you buy it, or do you continue to research other brands and models? Now imagine the sign in the window offers both the $99 Sony and a $169 top-of-the-range Aiwa, also well below list price. Do you buy either of them, or do you postpone the decision and do more research? Dr Schwartz says that, when researchers asked they found that, in the first case, 66 per cent of people said they'd buy the Sony and 34 per cent said they'd wait. In the second case, 27 per cent said they'd buy the Sony, 27 per cent said they'd buy the Aiwa and 46 per cent said they'd wait.

There you have it—a single, attractive choice in case one, no probs. But widen the choice to two attractive options and, in the process, oblige people to make a difficult choice between price and quality, and more people shy off making any decision. Now imagine a third scenario. The one-day sale offers the $99

The pleasures of consumerism

Sony and an inferior Aiwa at the list price of $105. Here, the added option doesn't create conflict. The Sony is better than the Aiwa *and* it's on special. Not surprisingly, almost no one chooses the Aiwa. What is surprising, however, is that 73 per cent go with the Sony—compared with 66 per cent when it was offered by itself. 'So the presence of a clearly inferior alternative makes it easier for consumers to take the plunge,' Dr Schwartz says.

He concludes that the expansion of choice has three unfortunate effects: it means decisions require more effort, it makes mistakes more likely and it makes the psychological consequences of mistakes more severe. When people start having second thoughts and convince themselves they've jumped the wrong way, they suffer 'buyer's remorse'. But they can also suffer 'anticipated regret'—the fear that they *may* jump the wrong way—which produces not just dissatisfaction but paralysis.

Dr Schwartz divides consumers into two categories: 'maximisers' and 'satisficers'. Maximisers seek and accept only the best; satisficers settle for something that's good enough, and don't worry about the possibility there might be something better. They settle for 'better' over 'best'. The point is that widening choice wreaks far more dissatisfaction on maximisers than satisficers. The maximisers are obliged to devote far more time and effort to making decisions, but remain forever fearful that the best is still out there somewhere.

The fundamental problem with increased consumption, of course, is the speed with which humans adapt to their improved circumstances, which means the buzz we get from acquiring something never lasts as long as we expect it to—a lesson many of us never learn. Thus, while the gains from acquiring stuff are less than we expect, excessive choice also diminishes satisfaction by increasing the psychic costs of acquisition. It turns out that more is less. And part of the secret to a happy life may be less choice rather than more.

The psychologists' message about consumption isn't completely negative, however. In my reading I've discovered two contributions towards making our consumption more satisfying. Did you know, for instance, that you're likely to gain more satisfaction (or utility) from buying services than from buying goods? That's the useful conclusion of a paper by Dr Leaf Van Boven of the University of Colorado and Professor Thomas Gilovich of Cornell University.

Actually, they don't put it quite that way. They say that 'experiential' purchases—those made with the primary intention of acquiring a life experience—make people happier than material purchases. The good life, they say, is better lived by doing things than having things. They came to this conclusion after undertaking surveys and laboratory experiments in which they asked people how they felt about the two kinds of purchases. Note, however, that this applies not to poor people, but to people in developed countries with a fair bit of discretionary income—that is, you and me.

By 'experiential purchases' Van Boven and Gilovich mean paying to do things—go to a concert, go skiing, go on a holiday, even go out to dinner. By 'material purchases' they mean buying tangible objects—clothes, jewellery and all manner of 'stuff'. In a way, this is a surprising finding. When you've spent money on an experience, pretty soon you've got nothing tangible to show for it. When you buy something material, however, it lasts for years. So why should doing things be so much more satisfying than having things?

First, because experiences are more open to positive reinterpretation. When we look back on the things we've done, we tend to forget the minor annoyances (how hot it was, all the flies, busting to get to the toilet) and the boring bits. The experience takes on a rosy glow, becoming better in recall than it was in reality. We even laugh over misadventures we found most unpleasant at the time. In contrast, one of the core findings of the happiness research is that people quickly adapt to material advances. We soon get used to owning the new lounge suite and it becomes part of the furniture, so to speak. So we need continuous material purchases to maintain the same level of satisfaction.

Second, because experiences are more central to our personal identities. A person's life is the sum of their experiences. The accumulation of rich experiences thus creates a richer life. Third, because experiences have greater social value. We enjoy talking about our experiences much more than about our possessions. Talking about our experiences—including our shared experiences—is the stock in trade of our relationships with family and friends. And good relationships are strongly associated with happiness.

This finding about experiencing rather than possessing fits with a more subtle finding from another psychologist, Professor Martin Seligman of the University of Pennsylvania, in his wonderful book *Authentic Happiness*. Dr Seligman warns against the snare of pursuing 'shortcuts to pleasure'. Such as? Drugs, chocolate, loveless sex, shopping, masturbation, television and spectator sport.

The point is not that these things are necessarily bad for us, nor that we should give them up entirely. It's that they yield only the briefest surge of good feeling. Every wealthy nation produces more and more of these shortcuts, forms of instant pleasure that require a minimum of effort on our part. And that's what's wrong with them—they're too easy. They're passive rather than active. We seem to have been built in such a way that things requiring more effort yield more satisfaction. It's the old story: you get out what you put in.

Dr Seligman tells of an academic colleague who kept an Amazonian lizard as a pet in his lab. It would eat nothing he could think of to feed it—not lettuce, mango, ground meat, swatted flies. It was starving before his eyes. One day he offered it a ham sandwich. No interest. He began reading the paper, finished the first section and allowed it to slip to the floor on top of the sandwich. 'The lizard took one look at this configuration, crept stealthily across the floor, leapt onto the newspaper, shredded it, and then gobbled up the ham sandwich', Dr Seligman writes. It needed to stalk and shred before it would eat. And we turn out to be a bit like that.

How does Dr Seligman know we gain so little pleasure from these shortcuts? From the findings of extensive research by the noted psychologist Mihaly Csikszentmihalyi (which means Michael St Michael of Csik, a town in Transylvania). St Mike gave pagers to thousands of subjects and then beeped them at random times during the day and evening. Whenever they were beeped they had to record what they were doing and how they felt about it. It's from such research that we learn an unsettling fact: the average mood while watching sitcoms on television is mild depression. Reading a book, however, gets a tick. It's a lot less passive than being slumped in front of the box.

So what's the alternative to shortcuts to pleasure? In Dr Seligman's schema, what lies beyond the pleasures is the gratifications, which are not feelings but activities we like doing: reading, rock climbing, dancing, good conversation, volleyball or playing bridge, for example. The gratifications absorb and engage us fully. They block consciousness of self and felt emotion, except in retrospect ('Wow, that was fun!'). When we progress to the gratifications, however, we're still in the foothills of satisfaction. Beyond conventional consumption, in the search for the good life lies the meaningful life in which we use our strengths in the service of something much larger than we are.

CHAPTER 13
The shortage of time

I've long been fascinated by the subject of time, but frustrated that I never seem to get a moment to study what the philosophers, sociologists and economists have had to say about it. You don't think time a suitable subject for an economics writer like me? That just shows how little time you've spent thinking about it. The thing about time is that whether we're rich or poor we each get an identical allocation of it—24 hours in a day, seven days in a week—and its supply is fixed. That makes time scarce—a valuable commodity—and economics is the study of scarcity and how we can get round it. In any case, haven't you heard that time is money?

The problem of time's scarcity goes to the heart of the way capitalist economies are organised and the way they evolve. Indeed, capital gets its value from the fact that we use it to

The shortage of time

achieve more with our time. One of the main ways we save time is through the division of labour, which involves specialisation and exchange. Rather than each producing our own bread, shoes and baked beans, we specialise in producing something we think we're good at then, per the medium of money, we exchange what we've produced for what others have produced.

Specialisation leaves us better off because specialists take less time to do things than we would. That's partly because of their greater know-how, but also because they're in a position to use better equipment than we could. They exploit economies of scale not open to us. Economists' obsession with efficiency is all about increasing the amount we can get achieved in an hour. They call it raising our productivity. And one of the main ways we do this is by the use of more and better 'labour-saving' machines.

In his book *In Praise of Slowness*, Carl Honoré reminds us that in primitive agrarian societies people were less conscious of the time, with sunrise and sunset the main markers and the passing of the seasons being very important. It was with the move to a capitalist economy, and particularly the arrival of the industrial revolution, that we became ever more conscious of the rapid passage of time through the day. With the invention of town clocks, workers acquired fixed times to start and finish work—and a lunch break no longer than an hour.

Mr Honoré says the wind-up alarm clock was invented in 1876 and the spread of watches completed our enslavement. As the ability to know the time spread, so did inculcation of the great virtue of punctuality and public condemnation of the vice of being 'behind time'. Punctuality, of course, involves reducing the waste of other people's time. So it's just part of the never-ending drive to eliminate time-wasting and make our use of time ever more efficient.

What applies to our working lives has its parallels in our private lives. The longer the hours we work, and the more the number of families where both partners go out to work, the greater the pressure on us to raise the efficiency of our free time. Taking a leaf from our bosses, we invest in an ever-expanding assortment of time-saving machinery: washing machines, dishwashers, clothesdryers, refrigerators, freezers, ovens and microwaves. We save the time it takes to visit people by using telephones. We save the time it takes to write a letter by using email. We save the time it takes to find a phone box (or to wait for someone to reach home) by using mobile phones.

We even save time on our leisure by paying specialists to make our music for us and play our sport for us. We go to gyms with machines that allow us to move from walking to cycling to rowing without any loss of time. And we drive rather than walk to the gym to save time. Another way we save time is to buy the time of others. We pay people to mind our kids, vacuum our houses, wash and iron our clothes and mow our lawns. We buy pre-prepared meals, get take-away or visit restaurants.

But the funny things is, despite all the effort we put into saving time at work and at home, and even though modern technology allows us to use our time more efficiently than ever, we still feel pressed. Our lives are still rushed—perhaps more rushed than ever. We have no time to do all the many things we'd like to do, starting with spending more time with family and friends, and some of us feel quite stressed.

The shortage of time

Part of the problem is that, as Parkinson discovered, work expands to fill the time available. At work, bosses just keep piling it on. If there's any risk that someone might be getting it easy, the boss lays off staff until the workers remaining have a full plate. Sometimes people who are already stretched have to work even harder because of 'downsizing'.

At home, studies by time-use experts demonstrate that labour-saving devices don't (see Chapter 11). The washing machine took a lot of the effort out of laundry, for instance, but we responded to that by adopting higher standards of cleanliness and putting our clothes in the wash more often. Result: we still spend as much time on laundry as ever. Do mobile phones and email really save us time? No, because the volume of calls and correspondence has expanded so enormously. Email messages can be dispatched to multiple recipients so easily they've become a major time-waster.

As for paying others to do the work around the house, it's not all it's cracked up to be either, because of what economists call the 'tax wedge'. You have to pay tax on the income you earn before you pay for child care or for household helpers, but the money you pay them isn't tax deductible. So unless your hourly wage rate is a lot higher than theirs, you end up having to work just to pay the wages of the people who leave you free to work.

Doesn't seem to be getting us far, does it? As Mr Honoré remarks, we find ourselves expected to 'think faster, work faster, talk faster, read faster, write faster, eat faster, move faster'. He says the whole world's suffering from 'time-sickness', a disease discovered by the American physician Larry Dossey, which is the obsessive belief that 'time is getting away, that there isn't enough of it, and that you must pedal faster and faster to keep up'.

Some of us find the fast pace of life exhilarating. Cities move faster than country towns and those who prefer the faster-paced life tend to congregate in cities. Why are we like this? Because the human species is innately competitive, and many of us are addicted to racing. But even if some of us don't consciously seek out the rapid life, we've gone along with it. And this gives rise to various modern maladies.

It's a safe assertion that people have never been more impatient—a condition that breeds dissatisfaction. In the great rush, we can't bear being held up. We hate cooling our heels in queues and waiting rooms and get inwardly agitated. Research shows that commuting—which means suffering a delay while moving from activity A to activity B—is our least pleasant daily experience.

The most extreme form of impatience is road rage. And it's not necessary to jump out of your car with a tyre lever to be afflicted with it. Most of us are. We travel with mindless impatience to get where we're going and with an impoliteness we wouldn't dream of exhibiting in other circumstances. We steadfastly refuse to let other drivers in when we have the right of way and, behind our closed windows, curse the supposed failings of other motorists.

A second speed-related malady is boredom—a condition that, according to Mr Honoré, hardly existed in earlier times. We've become so accustomed to continuous stimulation that we can't bear it when the stimulation stops. If we're forced to wait for more than a minute or two we simply must find something to read or

The shortage of time

listen to. We watch hours of indifferent television because we need relaxation, but can't bear to do it by just 'being'.

Doing nothing isn't a crime, it's an art—an art we've lost. We can't be alone with ourselves.

We're so rushed we're losing the ability to look forward to things. It's true. I remember that when I was about to take some long-service leave and go to Britain on a fabulous holiday, I was so frantic doing all that had to be done before I left that I had no time to contemplate how great it was going to be. It's possible to go to the other extreme, of course, and live your entire life looking forward to what's next. What's happening at present isn't of any interest, but what's coming up will be wonderful. Another ability we're losing, in other words, is being able to enjoy the moment. Since our lives consist of a string of moments, this is a sad way to be. Once in our grasp, the thing we've looked forward to becomes ordinary.

In the haste of life, we often neglect what we know matters most to us: family and friends. Why? Partly because, with the exception of little Katie's solo at the school concert, family and friends don't come with deadlines attached. They're not pressing. They'll always be there, so they can be pushed aside by things we imagine *are* pressing.

But why are we in such a tearing hurry, anyway? Because, says Mr Honoré, all the world's a store, and all the men and women merely shoppers. 'Tempted and titillated at every turn, we seek to cram in as much consumption and as many experiences as possible,' he says. 'As well as glittering careers, we want to take art courses, work out at the gym, read the newspaper and every book on the bestseller list, eat out with friends, go clubbing, watch hours of television, listen to music, spend time with the family, buy all the newest fashions and gadgets, go to the cinema, enjoy intimacy and great sex with our partners, holiday in far-flung locations and maybe even do some meaningful volunteer work.'

This is where our capitalist economy has led us astray. As we've seen, conventional economics is about helping us overcome the problem of time's scarcity. But despite all the ingenious means the economy offers to help us 'save time', we never end up with time to spare. Why not? Because economics is about trying to reconcile our limited time with our infinite wants. It does so by trying to cram as many of our wants as possible into our 24-hour days. Its single answer to the problems of modern life is: run faster.

Increasingly, however, we're getting to be like the fat man in the pie-eating contest, trying to jam as many pies into our faces as possible. We're not enjoying it one bit, but we're determined to win. We've got terribly muddled between means and ends, and we're substituting quantity for quality, convinced that 'more' equals 'better'.

So what can we do to improve the situation? Well, the first thing is to realise we're on a treadmill and, no matter how fast we run, it's not taking us anywhere we want to go. In which case, what's to be lost by running a bit slower rather than faster? What on earth is all the hurry? A question I like to ask myself is: why are we charging around as though we have only six months to live? If a personal goal is achieved by Friday rather than Tuesday, what would be lost?

I think we can train ourselves to be more patient. We can stay calm in queues, stop watching to see how fast the other queue's moving, just let our minds wander and see where it takes us. When you're commuting by bus or train, just watch the scenery as it passes—or observe the other passengers. When you're driving, accept that, in city traffic, hassling about speed gets you there no faster. We can train ourselves to be scrupulously polite: stop carrying on about other people's driving (it will only give us indigestion) and take pride in being the person who stops to let in someone stuck in a driveway.

We keep telling ourselves there's nothing we can do about all the work piled on us at the office, but how much is that just an excuse? Consider a study called 'The Time Pressure Illusion', by Robert Goodin of the Australian National University, with help from colleagues at the University of New South Wales's Social Policy Research Centre. Using the official survey of people's time use in 1992, the study looks at how much free time people aged 25 to 54 have left after taking account of their paid work, their unpaid household work and time devoted to 'personal care' (sleeping, washing, eating, etc.).

It found that individuals' average free time ranges from 36 hours a week (out of a total 168 hours in a week) for mothers in two-income households to 52 hours for men in childless, single-income couples. Most people have somewhere in the low 40s. The most striking result, however, is that people in two-income households have consistently less free time than people in other household types. That's true for both men and women, and whether or not they have children.

So here we have seeming proof of the increasing 'time pressure' most couples are under and the growing 'stress' involved in juggling work and family commitments. But this is where the study turns sneaky. Using quite austere and rather arbitrary standards, it calculates how much free time couples would have if they cut their work and personal-care time back to the bare minimum necessary to get by. (In the case of paid work, it assumes people cut their hours of work back to what would be needed to give them an income just above the poverty line—defined as half the median income.)

It finds that doing this would double the free time of two-income couples to 78 hours a week for each partner. So our perception of being under great time pressure is an illusion. Our lack of free time isn't unavoidable, it's voluntary. We're doing all this paid and unpaid work because we're trading our free time for a higher material living standard.

The moral of the story is not that we should all take a vow of poverty. Rather, we should stop complaining and acknowledge the price we've chosen to pay to be the proud owners of an ever-increasing quantity of 'stuff'—or, if we're genuinely unhappy with the present balance of our lives, we should take the steps within our power to calm things down a bit.

If we can't ease up on unpaid overtime for fear we'll lose that promotion, we should ask ourselves how much we need the promotion—especially if it means we'll have to run harder permanently. When it comes to how much we earn, we should realise there's a price to be paid for doing more work. If we're not willing to delay our purchase of a plasma screen TV, we shouldn't complain we've got no time to see the kids.

But, speaking of TV, that's an interesting question: if we're all so pushed for time, how come so many of us spend so much

The shortage of time

time watching television? Watching television is by far our biggest leisure activity. The typical Australian watches two to three hours of television a day. It seems that the reduction in working hours achieved in earlier decades has pretty much been replaced by TV watching.

It also seems, however, that many people watch more television than they consider to be good for them. It's reported that, in the United States, 40 per cent of adults and 70 per cent of teenagers admit they watch too much television. I dare say it's a thought that's crossed your mind. It's certainly one that has occupied mine at various times.

Why do so many of us have trouble exercising self-control over our television viewing? This is a question examined in a paper by the economist Bruno Frey and his colleagues at the Centre for Research in Economics, Management and the Arts at Basel in Switzerland. Professor Frey says many individuals are subject to a self-control problem, arising mainly because watching television offers immediate benefits whereas the costs are experienced only later. It's a question of the passage of time, you see: we suffer a lack of foresight.

Watching offers the benefit of entertainment and is considered by many of us to be one of the best ways of reducing stress. What's more, the *immediate* costs are negligible. You just have to push a button. 'In contrast to going to the cinema, the theatre or any outdoor activity, there is no need to be appropriately dressed before leaving the house, there is no need to buy a ticket and, in many cases, no need to reserve a seat in advance,' says Professor Frey. Watching television doesn't require any special physical or mental abilities and, unlike other leisure activities, it doesn't need to be coordinated with other people. It's quite possible to sit alone in front of the telly, while other leisure activities such as tennis or golf require a partner with similar time availability and similar preferences.

Watching telly does have costs, but Professor Frey notes that they're not experienced immediately and may not be predicted at all. 'The negative effects of not enough sleep, for example, only arise the next day,' he says. And the consequences of investing too little in social contacts, education or career take much longer to appear. A separate study finds that people who spend longer hours working also tend to spend longer hours watching television. Why? Because working long hours makes social contacts harder to organise, and this leads people to watch more television because it requires no effort at coordination.

Professor Frey quotes someone else's study of the effects of television, using a natural experiment involving a Canadian town that was unable to receive any TV signals until 1973 because of its location in a steep valley. In other respects it was similar to two nearby towns it was compared with. The study found that the introduction of television crowded out other activities, in particular those outside the home, such as sporting activities and visiting clubs. It reduced the reading abilities and creative thinking of children and fostered more aggressive behaviour and stereotyped ideas about gender roles.

The prof's own study used a sample of 42 000 people in 22 European countries in 2002–03. He found that the more television people watched, the less satisfied with their lives they tended to be. But this was only a correlation; it didn't say whether heavy

The shortage of time

television watching caused unhappiness, or unhappy people tended to watch more television. So, in an effort to shed more light on what was causing what, he looked deeper.

First he introduced the issue of opportunity cost. As we've seen, the thing about time is that if you spend it doing one thing, you can't spend it doing something else. The most attractive alternative use of your time is therefore the opportunity cost of your decision to do the first thing. But this means people's opportunity cost of watching television will vary with the alternative activities open to them. Some people—particularly the self-employed, managers and professionals, but also students—have the freedom to determine how long they work and how long they play. But other people have little choice and are expected to put in a fixed working week. Then there are people, such as the retired and the unemployed, who have greatly diminished demands on their time. You'd expect the time of those people free to switch between work and leisure to have a high opportunity cost, whereas the time of those people with little flexibility or no opportunity to work would have a low opportunity cost. You'd further expect it to be those people with a high opportunity cost of time who felt worst about watching too much telly.

And so it proved. Individuals in the group with high opportunity costs of time, who also watch more television than average, report lower life satisfaction. The subjective wellbeing of those who watch more than two and a half hours of television a day is significantly lower than that of people who watch less than half an hour a day. The size of the difference is as great as the difference in wellbeing between people who are without a partner and people who are married.

Professor Frey's second effort to discern cause and effect concerned television's effect on people's preferences and beliefs. Previous research has shown that heavy television viewing affects people's beliefs and preferences because life portrayed on television differs markedly and systematically from real life. TV programs contain much more violence and chaotic relationships and show many more affluent people and more luxury than exist in real life. People who spend a lot of time watching television thus tend to overestimate crime rates, to show more anxiety and less trust in others. They overestimate the affluence of others, report higher material aspirations and rate their own relative income lower.

The prof's research confirms these findings. 'Heavy TV viewers report lower satisfaction with their financial situation, place more importance on affluence, feel less safe, trust other people less and think they are involved in less social activities than their peers,' he finds. These sad attitudes and the reduced wellbeing they lead to are part of the unanticipated long-term cost of heavy viewing.

But to return to our theme of time, television can be a trap. In moderation, it's fine. It's a good way for busy people to unwind and it's a form of leisure that's terribly easy to organise. But, particularly for the busy, heavy viewing is ultimately unsatisfying and actually reduces our happiness. Even work will often be a more satisfying use of our time, but better still is leisure that requires more effort on our part and recognises our need to be the social animals nature made us.

CHAPTER 14
The attack on leisure

One of the most enticing words in the English language must surely be 'leisure'. What connotations of pleasure it conjures up! What visions of relaxation and enjoyment. Leisure is such an innately attractive thing that you might expect the role of a public commentator to be to warn against its excess. Back to work! Remember your duty! You've got a family to provide for! Have you no ambition? Sadly, ambition seems to have taken over, and leisure is under attack and in retreat. Society's problem these days is too little leisure, not too much. The attack on leisure is being led by business people and politicians, always in the name of economic progress. The economics, however, is bogus—a distortion of conventional economic principles pushed by workaholic businessmen (the women mostly have more sense). Sit back and let me attempt to put leisure back on its throne.

I hadn't realised until I read something by the Nobel laureate Robert Fogel that leisure is an invention of the 20th century. Until the beginning of that century, leisure was in very short supply in the industrialised countries. As the iconoclastic American economist Thorstein Veblen pointed out at the time in his *Theory of the Leisure Class* (published in 1899), leisure was 'conspicuously consumed' (his phrase) only by a small upper class. The typical person laboured for over 60 hours a week and had many chores at home which consumed an additional 10 or 12 hours. Aside from sleep, eating and hygiene, such workers usually had barely two hours a day for leisure.

Although opera, theatre and ballet performances were available, they were too expensive to be consumed ordinarily by the labouring class. Over the first half of the 20th century, however, hours of work fell by about a third. And the century saw a vast increase in the supply and the quality of leisure-time activities for the working class: movies, records, radio, television, videos, amusement parks, participant and spectator sports, and travel. But as the 21st century gets going, people are having their gains in leisure rapidly eroded.

Some people see leisure as the very antithesis of economics. But if that's what you think, you're the victim of business propaganda. Conventional economics has always recognised the value and virtue of leisure, seeing leisure as the antithesis not of economics, but of work. You see that in the concept beloved of elementary economic textbooks—the 'backward-bending labour supply curve'. The simplest economic analysis defines leisure merely as 'non-work'. It assumes that we derive utility from leisure, but disutility from work.

The attack on leisure

From this comes the startling discovery that people are only prepared to work for money. To induce them to give up an hour of leisure, they have to be paid income. They use this income to purchase goods and services, from which they derive a different kind of utility. As the hourly wage rate on offer increases, the more hours of labour people are prepared to supply (and the more hours of leisure they're prepared to give up). But after the hourly wage rate has reached a certain (high) point, the process goes into reverse. A rise in the wage rate prompts people to do less work, not more. And the higher the wage rate goes, the less work they do.

Why? Because the more leisure you give up, the more valuable your remaining leisure becomes. What's more, when your hourly wage rate rises, you can actually earn the same total income while working fewer hours. (In the jargon, the income effect overwhelms the substitution effect.) So you see that, although business people preach (and practice) workaholism, it's not part of the economists' gospel. Business people believe we should all be working longer, but economists don't—or, at least, shouldn't.

It's all about getting sorted in your mind about means and ends. Every economy is about production and consumption. Goods and services have to be produced if they're to be consumed. Because they're engaged in the production end of the process, business people tend to see production as an end in itself. Consumption is just something that's necessary to keep the wheels of industry turning—to provide the profits and stop inventories piling up.

Economists, on the other hand, emphasise that the objective is consumption. Production is merely the means to that end. We produce more simply so we can consume more. But even that isn't quite right. Though economists seem to be losing sight of the point, consumption, as such, isn't the ultimate objective. As chapter one of every economics text makes clear, the ultimate objective of economic activity is to maximise the community's utility—its feeling of satisfaction. Too often, economists take the logical shortcut of equating consumption with utility.

It's true, of course, that consumption yields utility. But here's the trick: so does leisure. Leisure yields utility for no reason other than that we enjoy it. Leisure is an economic good—in both senses of the word 'good'. So economic arguments that fail to recognise the intrinsic value of leisure will lead us to wrong conclusions. Conclusions that fail to maximise our utility.

When you think about it you realise that consumption without leisure yields little utility. Our utility comes not from buying things, but from using and enjoying them after they've been bought. But that use and enjoyment requires time—otherwise known as leisure. There are business people rich enough and silly enough to buy yachts and holiday homes they have no time to enjoy, but they're in the minority.

So it's leisure that keeps production and consumption in balance. If we were too busy working to have much time for leisure, we'd have less motive to consume. As well, with inadequate time to recuperate, the quality of our work effort would suffer. But to acknowledge leisure's essential role in the efficient functioning of the economy is to point to its extrinsic virtues. The real point is that leisure is intrinsically virtuous: it's a good thing merely because we enjoy it.

The attack on leisure

One aspect of the gospel of workaholism is the attempt to make us feel guilty about taking the odd public holiday. This was one of Jeff Kennett's specialties in Victoria. What are all these public holidays doing for Australia's international competitiveness? If guilt's what you're feeling—ignore it. The guilt is inconsistent with the most elementary economics, not to mention real life.

For a start, Australia didn't invent the public holiday. Every country has them and our 10 days a year are no more than average among the developed countries. Even the Americans take 10 and the nose-to-the-grindstone Japanese actually take 15. Similarly, our 20 days of annual leave is nothing to write home about. The Europeans almost invariably take a lot more than that—the Dutch come top with 31 days—and the Japanese and Americans aren't far behind us on 18 and 17 days respectively. When you put it all together and look at the average number of hours worked per employed person in 2000, we actually come top with 1855 hours a year. That's about 200 hours—or five working weeks—a year more than the average for the 17 OECD countries.

So if it ever was true that Australians lived in the land of the long weekend, it certainly isn't today.

A more significant objection to the fuss about public holidays is that, if you take maximising our production of goods and services to be the object of the exercise (as some silly business people and politicians seem to), working harder—that is, longer—isn't a sensible way to go about it. You don't understand the first thing about how the rich countries got to be rich, and will go on getting richer, if you think they did it by working harder. Rather, they did it by working smarter—a little smarter every year.

How do you get workers to work smarter? In the way we've been doing since before the industrial revolution: by giving them more and better machines to work with. By giving them an extra pair of hands, so to speak. This means developing and applying new technology and investing in more capital equipment. In these days of the IT revolution, however, we've become more conscious of the need to work smarter by increasing our investment in 'human capital'—the knowledge and skills our workers carry around in their heads. The more the developing countries take over the world's production of manufactured goods, with China at their head, the clearer it becomes that our future lies in using increased investment in education, training and lifelong learning to raise the skill levels of our workforce—something we're not doing well enough at present.

To put all this another way, if the nation's interest is in amassing worldly wealth, you don't focus on production (output), you focus on productivity (output relative to inputs). Any fool can increase output by increasing inputs (including hours worked). The genius of the capitalist economy is its long-proven ability to increase the output of goods and services much faster than the increase in inputs. This economic magic is achieved by technological advance, backed up by the accumulation of physical and human capital. Seen in this light, the question of how many days a year we take off pales into insignificant penny-pinching.

But there's a much more fundamental objection to the attempt to make us feel guilty about holidays: as we've seen, it confuses means and ends. The production of goods and services is a means to an end, not an end in itself. The end is what economists call

The attack on leisure

utility and the rest of us call happiness. And the point is that utility derives from a combination of consumption and leisure. Part of the key to happiness is contrast and striking the right balance between work and leisure. You'd expect neither the person who never stopped working nor the person who never worked to be particularly happy.

The defenders of capitalism are always telling us we should produce more because the richer we are, the more we can afford to do what we want—to spend money on fixing the environment, for instance. But here the same people are telling us we can't afford to take a few days off because we have to keep working and getting richer. This is muddleheaded. It takes the end of leisure and reduces it to a means to the end of increased production. It tries to make us into misers, who think the fun comes from making and counting money, not from spending it. It's like being too busy preparing a meal to sit down and enjoy it.

Although this is the most elementary and conventional economics, the funny thing is that economists regularly foster the misconceptions of business people and politicians by using a nation's total production of goods and services (GDP) divided by its population as the standard measure of its prosperity and economic success. The trouble with this approach is that it focuses on production rather than productivity. It thus implicitly assumes that the person who slaves night and day to amass goods and services is more successful, and happier, than the person who sets a high value on leisure—even where that person has high productivity, meaning they can well afford to take time off.

For years this measure of GDP per person has been used to show the Americans are far richer than the Europeans and to conclude there's something wrong with the European economy that needs 'reform'. But recent research has demonstrated that Europe's level of productivity is actually similar to America's, meaning that the Yanks' higher GDP per person is largely a product of their decision to take shorter holidays and generally work longer hours. The Europeans prefer more leisure and less work. It's a free choice. Despite all the propaganda we hear from the workaholics, there's nothing in orthodox economics that says the Americans have done the right thing and the Europeans the wrong thing. Nothing in common sense, either.

Next battleground in the attack on leisure is the Howard Government's industrial relations 'reform' permitting workers to cash in up to two weeks of their accrued annual leave. And the likelihood that some workers will be happy to do so is merely a reminder that most of us are guilty of putting too much emphasis on work at the expense of leisure and, in consequence, family life. Of failing to achieve a sensible balance in our lives.

Think about paid annual leave. It's an expense governments have forced on employers, starting with one week in 1941 and rising to four weeks in 1973. With what justification? It's obvious. People with full-time jobs need a decent break for rest and (literally) re-creation. Those with intellectually or emotionally demanding jobs need it, and so do people with jobs that are physically demanding. We also need time for extended, relaxed interaction with our children during school holidays. If the justification for this imposition on employers hasn't diminished—and I'd say that with intensification of work and the quickening pace of life it's actually increased—where on earth is the justification for letting people take the money, not the leave?

To say, as some politicians and employer groups do, that it makes the labour market more 'flexible' and gives workers greater 'choice' is to reveal that your values are out of kilter. What it says is that, as a society, we're putting ever more emphasis on production and consumption, and ever less on leisure and wellbeing. Why would employers be happy to see workers taking money rather than leave? To maintain production. Why would workers want to take the money? To spend it on additional consumption—or pay off debts from previous consumption.

Of course, a factor contributing to the temptation is that many workers have accrued large amounts of leave. According to a survey Woolcott Research conducted for See Australia in 2002, 30 per cent of workers hadn't taken any annual leave in the previous 12 months and another 50 per cent hadn't taken all their leave. In other words, only one worker in five uses all their leave. Among those who hadn't taken a holiday in the past 12 months, a quarter gave as their main reason 'too busy at work', while a further 8 per cent said they couldn't take time off because they were self-employed. By contrast, only 14 per cent said they couldn't afford it (even though those who did get away put the total cost of their holiday at well over $2000).

Among those who hadn't taken a holiday, 38 per cent said that 'at this stage of my career I can't afford to spend time away from work' and a similar proportion said that 'as a key person at work I feel it's my responsibility not to take too many holidays'. Again, among those who hadn't taken a holiday in the past 12 months, two-thirds said it was at least 18 months since they'd spent three or more nights away from home. And almost half said they had no current plan to take such a break. I'd say that if any further government intervention on leave is called for, it should be a new condition: use it or lose it.

As we've seen, the economists' standard model puts a lot of emphasis on the value of leisure. That's in theory. In practice, it's always being overlooked, partly because of economists', politicians' and business people's mania for judging progress solely in terms of the growth in GDP—for putting production and consumption ahead of wellbeing.

Remember how, in the 1970s, people used to foresee enormous reductions in working hours and wonder how on earth we were going to occupy all that leisure time? What a joke, when you consider how much longer and harder so many of us work these days! Whatever happened to that crazy idea? I'll tell you. We could have had significantly reduced working hours—we had the improvement in the productivity of labour to allow us to afford it—but we chose not to. I've no doubt that many production-obsessed bosses are happy with the way it's gone: everyone—well, most of us—working longer and harder for real wages that are very much higher than they were 30 years ago.

But, equally, I've no doubt that, had most workers preferred shorter hours to higher real wages—greater buying power—that's the way it would have gone. We opted for the money, not the leisure. Why? Because—with a fair bit of help from all the advertising and marketing to which we're subjected—we've acquired an addiction to material goods. Much of this involves our

The attack on leisure

self-defeating struggle to achieve social status—or at least avoid losing it—through our conspicuous consumption.

Psychological research shows that we're not as rivalrous about the holidays we take as we are about our clothes, cars, homes and children's schools. In consequence, we 'consume' too little leisure for our own good. As part of this, we've come increasingly to think of leisure as something you buy rather than something you have or do. Partly because we're so busy and partly because leisure equipment—from boats to the latest electronic doodad—can be used to display our status, leisure has become more capital-intensive and less labour-intensive. Music-making is something you do with a stereo, a walkman, a CD player or an iPod, it's not a noise you make yourself with your friends. Sport is something you watch on your home theatre, not something you play.

The latest gear is so expensive that we work—give up leisure—to buy the leisure equipment we don't have the leisure to enjoy. I saw an economist quoting as a laudable example of increased choice the worker who cashed out his annual leave so he could buy a plasma TV. Capital-intensive leisure tends to be more solitary—watching TV, playing computer games or surfing the net—whereas labour-intensive leisure tends to involve more interaction with family and friends. Capital-intensive leisure also tends to be more passive, adding to the community's growing problems with obesity, high blood pressure and diabetes.

The final battleground in the attack on leisure is the weekend. Slowly but steadily, without any of us quite realising what's happening, the weekend is being abolished—and all in the name of progress. It's occurring as a result of the deregulation of shopping hours and employers' use of workplace bargaining to 'buy out' weekend penalty rates. It's likely to progress a lot further now John Howard's industrial relations changes make the removal of penalty rates much easier.

Most business people and economists would say this trend is a jolly good thing. But what's so bad about the weekend that we'd like to get rid of it? Well, that's actually part of the problem. The weekend is nice, and no one's claiming otherwise. It's just that so many people would like to take a bite out of it. The more bites they take, the more the weekend fades away. What's nice about weekends is that families and friends can spend a lot more time together when everyone takes the same days off work or school. When people take different days off, groups have a lot more trouble getting together and we end up having less social contact.

So why is the weekend being eroded? Various forces are at work. One is that the productivity of factories, buildings and machines is raised if, rather than having them working for only 40 hours a week, you can keep them open and churning out product for something approaching three shifts a day, seven days a week. That's assuming you can find buyers for all the extra stuff you're churning out, of course. Which is why I often wonder why retailers are so keen on extended shopping hours.

How can they be sure that, by keeping their shops open for a much larger part of the week, they'll sell more stuff than they would have with shorter hours? I'm not convinced they do sell more. I know of no evidence that consumer spending has been growing faster than the economy generally since the advent of weekend trading a decade or more ago. Maybe retailers stay open all week for fear of losing business to competitors who already do. Or maybe the big retail chains and shopping centres expect that extended hours will allow them to win business away from smaller suburban shops.

The politicians claim that, by permitting longer opening hours, they're providing greater 'choice': shops don't need to stay open if they don't find it profitable, shoppers don't need to shop if they don't want to. Of course, the retailers would say they're merely responding to the demand from customers. Weekend shopping has proved very popular. And I don't doubt they're right—which is why it would be wrong to portray the invasion of the weekend as solely the work of the grasping capitalists. And the rise of the two-income household would have to be a significant factor. When both partners work, being able to shop on Saturday afternoons and Sundays is a great convenience. Indeed, it's one of the things that helps make two-income families workable.

But I think the phenomenon has more to it than that. I think the decline of the weekend is an unintended consequence of our intensifying materialism. We need shops to be open—and other people to be working—all weekend because of the rise of shopping as a leisure activity. We need clubs, restaurants, casinos and suchlike to be open all weekend because of our increasing tendency to *buy* our entertainment rather than make it ourselves with our family and friends.

It's part of our growing preference for working long hours, earning lots of money and paying people to do for us the things we no longer have the time or energy to do for ourselves. For many of us, earning and spending have become more important than leisure time and relationships.

But there's something logically inconsistent, even hypocritical, about all this. We want *our* weekends to be free of work, but other people to be working to meet our need to shop or be entertained. To some extent we're moving to a two-class society: the upper class who can afford not to work on weekends and the lower class who can't. But I doubt if even that dichotomy can last. Eventually the demands of bosses and consumers may mean almost all of us have to work weekends, and hope that the weekdays we get off happen to coincide with those of someone we know. By then we'll have reached materialist nirvana: we'll be living to work rather than working to live.

CHAPTER 15
Happiness

If you say you don't like the way economic rationalism is changing our country, you haven't quite put your finger on the problem. If you object to the increasingly mercenary behaviour of big business, you're missing the point. It took me ages to realise it, but these are just symptoms—outward manifestations of something a lot deeper. To understand the root cause of your dissatisfaction you have to appreciate that we're living through an era of heightened materialism.

There's nothing new about materialism, of course. A concern about money and material things has always been part of our makeup. But sometime over the past 20 or 30 years we suddenly became a lot more preoccupied with money than we had been. Materialism is the dominant characteristic of our era. Our descendants will look back on the last part of the 20th century and the early part of the 21st as The Age of Materialism. That's true not just for Australia, but for countries throughout the developed world. Claims about changes in people's values are hard to prove, but a leading American social psychologist, David Myers, of Hope College, Michigan, has produced impressive evidence for the United States.

In a poll that regularly asked people what factor was most important in a job, 'high income' rose to second highest in importance between the early 1970s and the early 1980s. Now consider the evidence from the American Council on Education's annual surveys of over 200 000 newly entering college students. Asked about their reasons for going to college, the percentage agreeing that an important one was 'to make more money' rose from half in 1971 to almost three-quarters by 1990. And the percentage believing it 'very important or essential' that they become 'very well-off financially' rose from 39 per cent in 1970 to 74 per cent in 1990. Over the same period, the percentage who began college hoping to 'develop a meaningful philosophy of life' slumped to 43 per cent, down from 76 per cent. This reversal stayed unchanged throughout the 1990s. Professor Myers calls this cultural shift 'the greening of America'. And though our bank notes are multicoloured, I don't doubt it's true of Australia, too.

The point is that, once you appreciate the way our values have changed, the reason for a lot of developments becomes clear. It's largely due to the recent rise of economic rationalism. Economists had been giving politicians the same advice, about the need to cut protection and reduce government regulation, for many decades. It's standard textbook stuff. And for decades

Happiness

the politicians unfailingly brushed aside such doctrinaire and politically unpopular advice.

Beginning in the early 1980s, however, the pollies started saying yes, and economic rationalism became the dominant ideology in the public sector. Why? Because the pollies were reacting to the electorate's increased materialism. They believed the public wanted them to make our economy more efficient at producing goods and services so as to raise our material standard of living more quickly. You have to admit that the politicians and their rationalist advisers have been strikingly successful. Their reforms have worked. The 1990s saw faster growth in productivity and real income per person than in any decade since the 1960s. (There's been only a slow reduction in unemployment, you say? True—but that wasn't a core objective.)

But there's been another development, one arising more from the changed behaviour of business than from government policy changes: the way money has invaded parts of our lives where it formerly played a lesser role. The most glaring case is sport. The big media companies have taken over and professionalised first cricket, then the various football codes. The taxpayer and corporate sponsors have poured millions into our Olympic athletes to beef up their medal-winning performance and, in the process, make them professionals. We're even seeing the commercialisation of schoolboy sport as some GPS schools use under-the-table scholarships to buy success. It's so simple. How do you win the comp? Apply a liberal dollop of money.

As we saw in the previous chapter, another institution that's been commercialised is the weekend. We used to stay at home or

233

visit friends, but now we shop or visit restaurants and commercial entertainment venues. This, of course, means more of us have to work on weekends. Heightened materialism explains why we've become more litigious. If we have some kind of accident, our first thought is: how can I turn my misfortune into cash? Here's my chance to get among the big money.

Even politics has been commercialised. The parties' election advertising battles require ever-growing millions. The big taxpayer election subsidies the pollies granted each other's parties have proved inadequate, so they're becoming increasingly beholden to union and business donors. And one result of political commercialisation is that politicians, bureaucrats and political staffers are cutting short their careers of service to the public so they can sell the expertise they've gained to the highest private-sector bidder.

Heightened materialism helps explain why the nation's CEOs have been awarding themselves unprecedented pay rises and why they've become much more hardnosed in their attitudes towards customers and employees. Heightened materialism also explains the declining ethical standards among company directors and auditors. And even our charities have been commercialised—these days, most sell their services to government.

Materialism is highly seductive and highly contagious. When you see your neighbours getting in for their chop, it's hard to resist the temptation to get in for yours. So all of us have been infected to a greater or lesser degree. It's so insidious even many of our clerics have failed to detect its rising influence. Or maybe they're not game to challenge it for fear of offending too many parishioners. Either way, they don't inveigh against greed and envy, but stick to fighting less controversial evils such as homosexuality and women priests.

Among the rest of us, it's OK to attack evil economic rationalists, greedy businessmen or stupid politicians, but it's just not done to attack materialism. That's altogether too close to home. To criticise materialism is to turn both sides against you. The Right sees it as an attack on the rich, while the Left sees it as an attempt to con the poor into accepting the bum hand they've been dealt. But the next time you're tempted to blame all your woes on economists or politicians or big business, pause and consider this: maybe the real trouble is that materialism isn't all it's cracked up to be.

But considering how noticeably more materialistic we've become—and the price we've paid for that change in priorities—there's an obvious question that deserves more attention than we give it: does money buy happiness? It's a question to which we each have our own answer, but it's also a question to which psychologists—and, increasingly, economists—are devoting much research. Happiness is one of the hot research topics in the social sciences.

And the answer is? Though surveys show that, when asked, most people say they don't believe money buys happiness, the research contradicts them: yes, it does. As you may suspect, however, there's a catch: the research also shows that money buys happiness with ever-decreasing effectiveness. In the jargon of economics, increasing income suffers from 'diminishing marginal utility'. (As an example, you experience DMU when you get less enjoyment from your third ice-cream than your second.)

The research findings on the relationship between income and 'subjective wellbeing' (as the scientists prefer to call it) are summarised in an article by Bruno Frey and Alois Stutzer, of the University of Zurich, in the prestigious *Journal of Economic Literature*. The first finding is that, on average, people living in rich countries report higher levels of happiness than those living in poor countries. But though there's a clear distinction between rich countries and poor, if you examine just the rich countries you find the correlation breaks down. In other words, just because rich country A is a bit wealthier than rich country B it doesn't mean the people living in A will feel happier than those living in B. What this suggests is the shocking idea that income isn't the only factor influencing people's feelings of satisfaction with life.

The second research finding is that, at a point in time in a particular country, those people with more income tend to be happier than those with less. But the difference between them is surprisingly small. Here I'm able to report some recent local research. The Australian Unity Wellbeing Index is based on a survey of about 11 000 people in all states, conducted over several years to 2005 by Professor Bob Cummins and his colleagues at Deakin University. People in the lowest income group (under $15 000 a year in household income) had an average satisfaction level of 72 per cent, whereas those in the highest group (more than $150 000 a year) had a level of 79 per cent. So there's an undeniable gradient, but it's remarkably gentle. As incomes rise, it takes progressively bigger increases to 'buy' an extra percentage point of satisfaction. That's diminishing marginal utility, all right. All this makes it likely that differences in income explain only a small proportion of the differences in happiness between people.

Happiness

The third research finding is that, in the developed countries, the strong growth in real income per person since the 1950s has led to little or no increase in the average level of happiness. Take the case of the United States, as described by Professor Myers in *The Pursuit of Happiness*. Since 1957, Americans' real income has more than doubled, to US$40 000 (A$53 000) per person. This huge increase in affluence has seen Americans own twice as many cars per person and eat out more than twice as often as they used to. Such things as dishwashers, clothesdryers and air-conditioning are now ubiquitous, and many Americans enjoy microwave ovens, home computers and big-screen colour TVs as well.

So has all this made them a lot happier? It has not. The proportion reporting themselves 'very happy' has actually fallen a fraction, from 35 to 33 per cent. Similar findings have been made for Britain, other countries in Europe, and Japan. I hardly need to remind you that these findings cut the ground out from under the unquestioned assumption of our business people, economists and politicians that the more economic growth we can achieve the better off we are. We may be better off in the sense that we own more stuff, but that doesn't seem to make us any happier.

The obvious question is: why does money turn out to be so inefficient at increasing happiness? Why do we get so little bang per buck? A key explanation offered by the psychologists is the speed with which our expectations and aspirations adjust to changed circumstances. We get an initial surge of pleasure from a pay rise or from winning a car in a raffle, but it never lasts long. What at first was new and wonderful soon becomes what we're used to and have come to expect. Thus do yesterday's luxuries become today's necessities. But, as survey evidence confirms, most of us remain convinced that 'a little more money' would make us happier—even though it never has before. Psychologists call this phenomenon the 'hedonic treadmill'—we keep striving for more money, but achieving a higher income never delivers any lasting increase in our happiness.

Another part of the explanation is that what we seek is not so much higher absolute income as higher relative income. Which would you prefer: to participate in a 10 per cent pay rise for everyone at your work, or to be singled out for promotion with a 10 per cent pay rise attached? Most of us are hoping that by raising our income we'll be raising our social status—our position in the pecking order. Trouble is, this is a 'zero-sum game'. I can increase my satisfaction only at the expense of the people I manage to overtake. And even then my satisfaction is unlikely to last long. Why not? Because our aspirations are always upward-looking. No matter how many people we overtake, there's always someone doing better than we are.

A related factor may be that, because most of us managed to satisfy our basic needs for food, clothing and shelter a long time ago, we're spending an increasing proportion of our incomes on what economists call 'positional goods'—goods intended to demonstrate our superior position in society. Just about all the ordinary things we buy can be used as positional goods if we've a mind to: the labels on the clothes we choose, the way we dress young children and the brand of sneakers our teenagers wear, the class of restaurant we visit, whether our car is a late-model European job, the suburb we choose to live in and the schools we send our offspring to.

Happiness

Most of these things are hugely more expensive than the regular model—that's an essential part of their allure—but you have to doubt how much lasting satisfaction they bring. No matter how flash your car is, there's always someone with a better one. It seems to me that with our shift to hyper-materialism we are, as the old ad said, smoking more but enjoying it less.

But if all the research tells us money isn't particularly efficient at making us happy, what is? We all instinctively know the broad answer to that question: people are more important than things. So I know this is going to sound like a Hallmark greeting card (and hence do great damage to my reputation as a flint-hearted economic rationalist), but I'm going to stick strictly to research-based answers to the question. Some of the most striking research has been done by Tim Kasser, a psychologist at Knox College, Illinois, and is explained in his book, *The High Price of Materialism*.

His approach is to explore people's values—what they view as important in life—and measure the correlation with their feelings of wellbeing. His many careful studies consistently find that people with materialistic values (those who give highest emphasis to the pursuit of money, possessions, personal appearance, or fame and popularity) report lower psychological wellbeing than people with less-materialistic values (those giving highest emphasis to self-acceptance and personal growth, intimacy and friendship, or contributing to society).

Professor Kasser refers to materialistic values as 'extrinsic'—they involve seeking satisfaction outside yourself. People with extrinsic values tend to be possessive (they prefer to own rather than rent and don't like throwing stuff away), 'non-generous' and envious. They also watch a lot of television—which makes them worse. They report more symptoms of anxiety, are at greater risk of depression and experience more frequent physical irritations. They use more alcohol and drugs and have more impoverished personal relationships. Even their dreams seem infected with anxiety and distress. 'Even the *successful* pursuit of materialistic ideals typically turns out to be empty and unsatisfying,' Professor Kasser says. Even *aspiring* to greater wealth is likely to be associated with increased personal unhappiness.

Among the many social scientists now working in the burgeoning field of happiness research, one of the leading scholars is Ed Diener, professor of psychology at the University of Illinois. Ask him what advice he'd give to people who want to be happy and, after a lot of academic disclaimers about no magic elixirs, etc., he nominates three 'steps people can take to ensure they are as happy as they can be'.

'First, we need good friends and family, and we may need to sacrifice to some extent to ensure we have intimate, loving relationships—people who care about us, and about whom we care deeply,' he says. This fits with several points made by David Myers in *The Pursuit of Happiness*. 'Give priority to close relationships,' Myers advises. 'There are few better remedies for unhappiness than an intimate friendship with someone who cares deeply about you. Confiding is good for soul and body.'

But don't all of us already know this? Yes we do, but we don't always give it priority. Another happiness guru, the American political scientist Robert Lane, writes that 'part of the materialist syndrome is the crowding out of companionship because of the precedence given to material pursuits. Materialists do, in fact, want "warm relationships with others"—they just do not give this goal a high priority.' Professor Myers offers some related advice: 'Focus beyond the self. Reach out to those in need. Happiness increases helpfulness—those who feel good, do good. But doing good also makes one feel good. Compassionate acts help one feel better about oneself.'

Professor Diener's second step towards a happier life is to involve yourself in activities—work, for example—that you enjoy and value. 'We are likely to be best at things we value and think are interesting,' he says. Professor Myers agrees. 'Seek work and leisure that engages your skills,' he says. Both men are reflecting the research findings of psychologist Mihaly Csikszentmihalyi, of Claremont Graduate University in Los Angeles, who has discovered a wonderful state of being he calls 'flow'.

To be in flow is to be unself-consciously absorbed in what you're doing. You forget yourself and don't notice the time flying by—you're happy. According to Myers, 'flow experiences boost our sense of self-esteem, competence and wellbeing'. Studies show a key ingredient of satisfying work is that it be challenging without being overwhelming. Your skills need to be engaged and tested. Mr C (the bloke with the unspellable name) found there are four ways to turn adversity or boredom into enjoyment: set goals, immerse yourself in the activity, pay attention to what's happening and enjoy the immediate experience. What applies to work applies equally to leisure. 'We all want to have more free time,' Mr C says, 'but when we get it we don't know what to do with it.' Be active: most people are happier gardening than sitting on a powerboat, or talking to friends than watching television.

Professor Diener's final step towards a happier life is to control how you look at the world. 'We need to train ourselves not to make a big deal out of trivial hassles, to learn to focus on the process of working towards our goals (not waiting to be happy until we achieve them) and to think about our blessings (making a habit of noticing the good things in our lives),' he says.

Professor Myers offers a couple more tips. 'Act happy,' he advises. 'Talk *as if* you feel positive self-esteem, are optimistic and are outgoing. Going through the motions can trigger the emotions. Join the "movement" movement. An avalanche of recent research reveals that aerobic exercise not only promotes health and energy, it also is an antidote for mild depression and anxiety. Sound minds reside in sound bodies. Give your body the sleep it wants. Happy people live active, vigorous lives, yet reserve time for renewing sleep and solitude. Many people suffer from a sleep debt, with resulting fatigue, diminished alertness and gloomy moods.'

Professor Myers, a Christian, slips in a commercial message (research-based, naturally): 'Take care of the soul. In study after study, actively religious people are happier. They cope better with crises. For many people, faith provides a support community, a sense of life's meaning, feelings of ultimate acceptance, a reason to focus beyond self and a timeless perspective on life's woes.'

Finally, let's return to our tendency to spend on positional goods to demonstrate our social status. In his book *Luxury Fever*, the economist Robert Frank, of Cornell University, argues that our preoccupation with spending on conspicuous consumption diverts us from items of 'inconspicuous consumption' that really would increase our satisfaction. If we spent less, we'd be able to work less and that would leave us free to 'spend' more on things that psychological studies show add to our feelings of wellbeing (as well as improving our health): getting adequate sleep, spending more time with our kids, enjoying the company of friends and doing regular aerobic exercise.

It seems pretty clear—to me, at least—that much of the pressure we put on governments to keep taxes low is motivated by our desire to have more disposable income to dispose on things we believe would bring us greater status. But Professor Frank argues that, if we were prepared to divert more of our income to governments, they could spend it on inconspicuous items more likely to bring us lasting satisfaction by raising our quality of life. Such as? Reducing traffic congestion and commuting time, reducing aircraft and other noise pollution, and improving air and water quality. The politicians aren't likely to start doing that, however, until they get a clear message from most of us that we're tiring of living in an era of hyper-materialism.

Last word: My take-home message

There's a last question to cover before I offer my take-home message: are we perpetrators or victims? Are we working so hard because we're mad materialists or because our occupations or our bosses leave us little choice? Are we volunteers or conscripts in the rat race? As cogs in the capitalist machine, how much choice do we get in the lives we lead? Let me tell you a story.

On a bushwalk with a neurologist mate the other day he mentioned that he'd just been to a good lecture on nature–versus–nurture. 'Oh great,' I said, 'so what's the latest—which side did they come down on?' 'The usual,' he replied, '50/50. It's always 50/50.' (And, indeed, that's the answer most psychologists give when asked if our happiness level is determined by our genes or our circumstances.)

Last word

So that's my answer to whether we're perpetrators or victims: a fair bit of both. The capitalist system *is* a system and it does promote and reward conformity. We *are* cogs in the machine and this does constrain our freedom of action. What the capitalists require of us is simple: produce, consume, die. While the economists' ideology proclaims 'consumer sovereignty'—the producers are there merely to wait upon the consumers' every wish—the producers maintain a barrage of advertising and other marketing to keep us spending. None of us is impervious to the blandishments of advertising, though some are more affected than others.

But I'm the son of a preacher and if you think I'm going to absolve you from personal responsibility you're much mistaken. Whatever the constraints, we must be masters of our own destiny. It's when all the individuals surrender their autonomy that the system really does take over. And it's when enough individuals resist that systems must accommodate them or face revolt.

I know enough psychology to understand that we're social animals. We care deeply what other people think of us, we like to fit in, hate being left behind and are comfortable when we're doing what everyone else is doing. We are also, however, thinking animals. We're not slaves and we can stand out from the crowd if we've got a good enough reason to. If you're conforming more but enjoying it less, consider stopping.

One thing economics has taught me is to avoid all-or-nothing thinking. Life is about trade-offs and the winners are people who've found the trade-off that most suits them. The choice we face is not between being a mindless company man and a hippy dropout in Nimbin. There are plenty of intermediate stops.

I suspect there's a lot of self-deception among those who assure us they'd like to spend more time with the kids but their financial pressures or the particular business they're in just won't permit it. Too often, all they're saying is they wish they could have their cake and eat it. Or they're making excuses to cover up the priorities they've picked. Life *is* about opportunity cost. We can't have it all; we do have to choose. And often the choices we make reveal our true preferences. We *would* like to spend more time with the kids, but we don't want it so badly that we'll settle for a slightly less comfortable lifestyle or risk losing our next promotion. We'd love to have more leisure time, but not so badly that we're prepared to curb our workaholism. There *is* a price to be paid for shifting to a more fulfilling, satisfying life. Don't let anyone convince you otherwise. But if you decide that price is too high, don't solicit sympathy over what you're missing.

OK, let me try to summarise this book's message. There's more to life than work and consumption. All of us know people are more important than things; our relationships are worth more to us than our possessions. But we live in an era where the material is crowding out the human. It's happening all around us—and it's easy to go along with the trend and hard to resist it.

But if we care about it enough there is much we can do, short of dropping out, to get a better balance into our lives. Consciously give your partner and children a higher priority. Don't be in such a tearing hurry. Opt for the simple pleasures. Control the television in your life. Take all your holidays and spend them with your kids. Stop trying so hard to display your status to the world. Be a little less concerned about keeping up with the neighbours. Let 'em

Last word

think they're beating you. The reward is less worry about money. Try to get into a job you can enjoy for its own sake. And here's the big one: experience the remarkable liberation of ceasing to care about your next promotion.

But above all, don't let people preach at you.

Bibliography

References are arranged in order of their appearance in each chapter.

Chapter 1   The changing workforce

Australian Bureau of Statistics (2003) 'Longer working hours', in *Australian Social Trends 2003*, catalogue no. 4102.0, Canberra.

Australian Bureau of Statistics (2006) *Household Expenditure Survey 2003/04*, catalogue no. 6530.0, Canberra.

Mark Cully (2002) 'The cleaner, the waiter, the computer operator: Job change, 1986–2001', *Australian Bulletin of Labour*, vol. 28, no. 3.

Layard, Richard (2003) 'Happiness: Has social science a clue?', Lionel Robbins Memorial Lectures, delivered on 3, 4, 5 March at London School of Economics.

Marmot, M., Kogevinas, M. and Elston, M.A. (1987) 'Social/ economic status and disease', *Annual Review of Public Health*, vol. 8, pp. 111–35.

Bibliography

Chapter 2   Women at work

Apps, Patricia (2004) 'High taxation of working families', in *Fairness and Services*, Australian Council of Social Service paper no. 136, Sydney.

McDonald, Peter (2002) 'Sustaining fertility through public policy: The range of options', *Population*, vol. 57, no. 3, pp. 417–46.

Chapter 3   The cost of kids

Richardson, Sue (2000) 'Society's investment in children', National Institute of Labour Studies working paper no. 151, Flinders University, Adelaide.

Ironmonger, Duncan (1996) 'Bringing up Betty and Bobby', in N.J. Taylor and A.B. Smith (eds), *Investing in Children: Primary prevention strategies social organisation of care*, Children's Issues Centre, University of Otago, New Zealand, pp. 27–42.

Australian Council of Social Service (2003) 'Poverty, policy and the cost of raising teenagers', ACOSS, Sydney.

Department of Social Security (1998) *Indicative Budget Standards for Australia*, AGPS, Canberra.

Tiffen, Rodney and Gittins, Ross (2004) *How Australia Compares*, Cambridge University Press, Cambridge.

Schneider, Judy (2000) 'The increasing financial dependency of young people on their parents', *Journal of Youth Studies*, vol. 3, no. 1, pp. 5–20.

Chapter 4   The value of higher education

Win, Rosemary and Miller, Paul W. (2005) 'The effects of individual and school factors on university students' academic performance', *Australian Economic Review*, vol. 38, no. 1, pp. 1–18.

GITTINOMIC$

Birch, Elisa Rose and Miller, Paul W. (2004) 'The determinants of students' tertiary academic success', paper delivered to Productivity Commission Conference, Canberra, October.

Borland, Jeff (2002) 'New estimates of the private rate of return to university education in Australia', working paper no. 14/02, Melbourne Institute, University of Melbourne.

Beer, Gillian and Chapman, Bruce (2004) 'HECS system changes: Impact on students', *Agenda*, vol. 11, no. 2, pp. 157–74.

Chapter 5   The Great Australian Home

Hamilton, Clive and Denniss, Richard (2005) *Affluenza*, Allen & Unwin, Sydney.

Reserve Bank of Australia (2003) 'Submission to the Productivity Commission Inquiry on First Home Ownership', occasional paper no. 16, Sydney.

Chapter 6   Saving, debt and guilt

Hamilton, Clive and Denniss, Richard (2005) *Affluenza*, Allen & Unwin, Sydney.

Reserve Bank of Australia (2005) *Financial Stability Review*, March, Sydney.

Chapter 7   Paying for health care

Australian Institute of Health and Welfare (2004) *Australia's Health*, Canberra.

Australian Institute of Health and Welfare (2003) *National Report on Health Sector Indicators*, Canberra.

Australian Institute of Health and Welfare (2005) *Health Expenditure Australia 2003/04*, Canberra.

Bibliography

Productivity Commission (2005) *Impacts of Medical Technology in Australia*, progress report, Melbourne.

Allen Consulting Group (2004) *Governments Working Together*, report prepared for the Victorian Government, Melbourne.

Chapter 8   Taxes—love 'em or hate 'em

Lloyd, Rachel, Harding, Ann and Warren, Neil (2005) 'Redistribution, the welfare state and lifetime transitions', paper presented at the conference on Transitions and Risk, Melbourne, 24 February, NATSEM, University of Canberra.

Michael Keating (2004) 'The case for increased taxation', policy paper no. 1, Academy of the Social Sciences in Australia, Canberra.

Chapter 9   Crime and drugs

Weatherburn, Don and Grabosky, Peter (1999) 'Strategy approaches to property crime control', *Policing and Society*, vol. 8, pp. 77–96.

Mayhew, Pat (2003) 'Counting the costs of crime in Australia', *Trends and Issues*, no. 247, Australian Institute of Criminology, Canberra.

Stevenson, R.J., Forsythe, M.V. and Weatherburn, D. (2001) 'The stolen goods market in New South Wales, Australia', *British Journal of Criminology*, vol. 41, pp. 101–18.

Weatherburn, Don (2004) *Law and Order in Australia: Rhetoric and Reality*, Federation Press, Sydney.

Moffatt, Steve, Weatherburn, Don and Donnelly, Neil (2005) 'What caused the recent drop in property crime?', *Crime and Justice Bulletin*, no. 85, NSW Bureau of Crime Statistics and Research, Sydney.

Moffatt, Steve and Poynton, Suzanne (2006) 'Long-term trends in property and violent crime in New South Wales', *Crime and Justice Bulletin*, no. 90, NSW Bureau of Crime Statistics and Research, Sydney.

Chapter 10   Our ageing population

Productivity Commission (2004) *Economic Implications of an Ageing Australia*, draft research report, Melbourne.

Australian Government (2002) *Intergenerational Report*, budget paper no. 5, 2002/03, Canberra.

Australian Government (2004) *Australia's Demographic Challenges*, Canberra.

Dowrick, Steve and McDonald, Peter (2002) *Comments on Intergenerational Report 2002/03*, mimeo, Australian National University, Canberra.

Schofield, Deborah and Beard, John (2005) 'Baby boomer doctors and nurses: Demographic change and transition to retirement', *Medical Journal of Australia*, vol. 183, no. 2, pp. 80–3.

Chapter 11   Housework has value

Bittman, Michael and Wajcman, Judy (1999) 'The rush hour: The quality of leisure time and gender equity', Social Policy Research Centre discussion paper no. 97, University of New South Wales, Sydney.

Bittman, Michael, Rice, James and Wajcman, Judy (2003) 'Appliances and their impact: The ownership of domestic technology and time spent on household work', Social Policy Research Centre discussion paper no. 129, University of New South Wales, Sydney.

Bibliography

Bittman, Michael, Meagher, Gabrielle and Matheson, George (1998) 'The changing boundary between home and market: Australian trends in outsourcing domestic labour', Social Policy Research Centre discussion paper no. 86, University of New South Wales, Sydney.

Ironmonger, Duncan and Soupourmas, Faye (2002) 'Calculating Australia's gross household product', Department of Economics research paper no. 833, University of Melbourne.

Ironmonger, Duncan (1995) 'Household industries', in Kim Sawyer and Joy Ross (eds), *The Changing Structure of Australian Industry*, McGraw-Hill, Sydney.

Chapter 12   The pleasures of consumerism

Hamilton, Clive (2003) *Growth Fetish*, Allen & Unwin, Sydney.

Schwartz, Barry (2004) *The Paradox of Choice*, Ecco/HarperCollins, New York.

Van Boven, Leaf and Gilovich, Thomas (2003) 'To do or to have: That is the question', *Journal of Personality and Social Psychology*, vol. 85, pp. 1193–202.

Seligman, Martin E.P. (2002) *Authentic Happiness*, Random House Australia, Sydney.

Chapter 13   The shortage of time

Honoré, Carl (2004) *In Praise of Slowness*, HarperCollins, New York.

Goodin, Robert, Rice, James, Bittman, Michael and Saunders, Peter (2002) 'The time pressure illusion: Discretionary time versus free time', Social Policy Research Centre discussion paper no. 115, University of New South Wales, Sydney.

Frey, Bruno S., Benesch, Christine and Stutzer, Alois (2005) 'Does watching TV make us happy?', Centre for Research in Economics, Management and the Arts working paper no. 2005–15, Basel, Switzerland.

Chapter 14   The attack on leisure
Veblen, Thorstein B. (1899) *The Theory of the Leisure Class*, reprinted Penguin Classics, 1994.

Chapter 15   Happiness
Myers, David G. (1991) *The Pursuit of Happiness*, William Morrow, New York.

Frey, Bruno S. and Stutzer, Alois (2002) 'What can economists learn from happiness research?', *Journal of Economic Literature*, vol. XL, pp. 402–35.

Australian Unity Wellbeing Index, <www.australianunity.com.au/au/info/wellbeingindex> accessed August 2006.

Kasser, Tim (2002) *The High Price of Materialism*, MIT Press, Cambridge, Massachusetts.

Diener, Ed (2006) Frequently asked questions, <www.psych.uiuc.edu/~ediener/faq.html> (accessed 15 March 2006).

Lane, Robert E. (2000) *The Loss of Happiness in Market Democracies*, Yale University Press, New Haven.

Frank, Robert H. (1999) *Luxury Fever*, The Free Press, New York.